Nelson
Mathematics 4
Workbook

Series Authors and Senior Consultants

Mary Lou Kestell • Marian Small

Workbook Authors

Anne Boyd • Carol Brydon • Andrea Dickson
Catharine Gilmour • Elizabeth Grill-Donovan • Jack Hope
Wendy Klassen • Kathy Kubota-Zarivnij • David Leach
Pat Margerm • Gail May • Pat Milot
Scott Sincerbox • Debbie Sturgeon • Rosita Tseng Tam

THOMSON
NELSON

Australia   Canada   Mexico   Singapore   Spain   United Kingdom   United States

THOMSON

NELSON

Nelson Mathematics 4 Workbook

Series Authors and Senior Consultants
Mary Lou Kestell, Marian Small

Workbook Authors
Anne Boyd, Carol Brydon,
Andrea Dickson, Catharine Gilmour,
Elizabeth Grill-Donovan,
Jack Hope, Wendy Klassen,
Kathy Kubota-Zarivnij, David Leach,
Pat Margerm, Gail May, Pat Milot,
Scott Sincerbox, Debbie Sturgeon,
Rosita Tseng Tam

Reviewers
Nancy Campbell,
(Rainbow Board of Education)
Anna Dutfield,
(Toronto District School Board)
Rose Scaini

Director of Publishing
David Steele

Publisher, Mathematics
Beverley Buxton

Senior Program Manager
Shirley Barrett

Workbook Program Manager
Janice Nixon

Editorial Assistant
Christi Davis

Executive Managing Editor, Development & Testing
Cheryl Turner

Executive Managing Editor, Production
Nicola Balfour

Senior Production Editor
Linh Vu

Copy Editor
Julia Cochrane

Production Coordinator
Franca Mandarino

Manufacturing Coordinator
Sharon Latta Paterson

Creative Director
Angela Cluer

Art Director
Ken Phipps

Art Management
ArtPlus Ltd., Suzanne Peden

Illustrators
ArtPlus Ltd.

Interior and Cover Design
Suzanne Peden

ArtPlus Ltd. Production Coordinator
Dana Lloyd

Composition
ArtPlus Ltd.

Printer
Webcom Limited

National Library of Canada Cataloguing in Publication Data

Nelson mathematics 4. Workbook / Mary Lou Kestell ... [et al.].

ISBN 0-17-620184-X

1. Mathematics—Problems, exercises, etc.
I. Kestell, Mary Louise II. Title: Nelson mathematics four.

QA135.6.N444 2003 Suppl. 1   510
C2003-904019-4

Contents

Message to Parent/Guardian

This workbook has one page of practice questions for each lesson in your child's textbook *Nelson Mathematics 4*. The questions in the workbook are similar to the ones in the text, so they should look familiar to your child. The lesson Goal and the At-Home Help on each page will help you to provide support if your child needs it.

At the end of each chapter is a page of multiple-choice questions called "Test Yourself." This is an opportunity for you and your child to see how well she or he understands.

You can help your child explore and understand math ideas by making available some commonly found materials, such as

- string, scissors, and a ruler (for measurement)
- counters such as bread tags or dry cereal (for number operations and patterns)
- packages, cans, toothpicks, and modelling clay (for geometry)
- grid paper, magazines, and newspapers (for data management)
- board game spinners, dice, and card games (for probability)

You might also encourage your child to use technology if it is available, such as

- a calculator (for exploring number patterns and operations)
- a computer (for investigating the wealth of information that exists on the Internet to help people learn and enjoy math)

Visit the Nelson Web site at **www.mathK8.nelson.com** to view answers and find out more about the mathematics your child is learning.

It's amazing what you can learn when you look at math through your child's eyes! Here are some things you might watch for.

Checklist
- ☑ Can your child clearly explain her or his thinking?
- ☑ Does your child check to see whether an answer makes sense?
- ☑ Does your child persevere until the work is complete?
- ☑ Does your child connect new concepts to what has already been learned?
- ☑ Is your child proud of what's been accomplished so far?

1 Patterns with Multiple Attributes

Goal Describe, extend, and create patterns that change in many ways.

1. **a)** Complete the pattern.

   ★★□○★★□○ ___ ___ ___

   b) Describe it. _____

   _____

   c) Write a letter model for it.

   _____

2. **a)** Complete the pattern.

   △▲○△▲○○ ___ ___ ___ ___ ___

   b) Describe it. _____

   _____

   _____

   _____

   _____

   c) Write a letter model for it. _____

3. Write a letter model for the pattern. _____

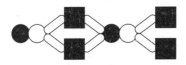

4. Create a pattern with at least 2 shapes and 2 colours.

At-Home Help

Patterns made with shapes can be
• described by the shapes and colours and how they change
• represented with a letter model

For example,

A black square is followed by a white triangle and then a white square. Then the shapes repeat.

A – B – C – A – B – C – A – B – C

---

2 Number Patterns

Goal Create, describe, and extend number patterns.

1. Describe each pattern. Write the next 3 numbers.

   a) 50, 54, 58, 62, 66, _____, _____, _____

   _____

   b) 45, 40, 35, 30, 25, _____, _____, _____

   _____

   c) 3, 6, 10, 15, 21, _____, _____, _____

   _____

   _____

2. Circle the letter of the statement that describes the pattern 8, 10, 13, 17, 22, 28.

   A. The numbers increase by the same amount each time.

   B. The numbers decrease by the same amount each time.

   C. The numbers increase by 1 more each time.

   D. The numbers increase by 2 each time.

3. Write another description for the pattern in Question 2.

   _____

   _____

4. Mary wants to increase her exercise time every day. She starts with 5 minutes and adds 5 minutes each day. How long will she exercise on the 7th day?

   a) Write the pattern. _____

   b) Describe the pattern. _____

   _____

   c) How long will she exercise on the 7th day? _____

3 Patterns in T-Charts

Goal Use t-charts to identify and extend patterns.

You will need coloured pencils or markers.

1. This ring has 4 birthstones—
ruby (red), sapphire (blue),
emerald (green), and ruby (red).

a) Colour the stones in this picture.

b) Complete the t-chart below to show how
many stones of all types are in 8 rings.

c) Look at the numbers in the 2nd column.
Write a pattern rule.

_____

_____

At-Home Help

A pendant has
these shapes.

This **t-chart** shows
how many ◇ are
in increasing
numbers of pendants.

Number of pendants	Total number of ◇
1	2
2	4
3	6
4	8
5	10

d) Complete the t-chart below to show how many ruby stones
are in 8 rings.

e) Look at the numbers in the 2nd column. Write a pattern rule.

_____

part b) Number of rings	Total number of stones	part d) Number of rings	Total number of ruby stones
1		1	
2		2	
3		3	
4		4	
5		5	
6		6	
7		7	
8		8	

4 Measurement Patterns

Goal Extend time patterns in t-charts.

1. Josef reads for 25 minutes each school night.

   a) Complete the t-chart below to show many minutes he read in 10 nights.

   b) Look at the numbers in the 2nd column. Write a pattern rule.

   _____

   _____

2. Lina takes piano lessons 4 times a month.

   a) Complete the t-chart below to find the number of piano lessons she takes in 1 year.

   b) Look at the numbers in the 2nd column. Write a pattern rule.

   _____

At–Home Help

George practises the piano for 15 minutes each day. This t-chart shows how many minutes he practises in increasing numbers of days.

Days	Total number of minutes
1	15
2	30
3	45
4	60
5	75

Question 1.

Days	Total number of minutes
1	
2	
3	
4	
5	
6	
7	
8	
9	
10	

Question 2.

Months	Total number of lessons
1	
2	
3	
4	
5	
6	
7	
8	
9	
10	
11	
12	

Solve Problems Using a Patterning Strategy

Goal Look for a pattern to solve a problem.

Show the events on the 100 chart using the mark indicated.

1. Every 2nd day the class has gym. Mark all the day numbers with \.

2. Every 3rd day the class has art. Mark all the day numbers with /.

3. Every 5th day the class has an hour of math games. Circle all the day numbers.

4. a) Describe the pattern of the days when the class has gym and art.

   _____

   _____

   _____

100 Days of School

1	2	3	4	5	6	7	8	9	10
11	12	13	14	15	16	17	18	19	20
21	22	23	24	25	26	27	28	29	30
31	32	33	34	35	36	37	38	39	40
41	42	43	44	45	46	47	48	49	50
51	52	53	54	55	56	57	58	59	60
61	62	63	64	65	66	67	68	69	70
71	72	73	74	75	76	77	78	79	80
81	82	83	84	85	86	87	88	89	90
91	92	93	94	95	96	97	98	99	100

   b) How many times in 100 days does the class have gym and art?

   _____

5. a) Describe the pattern of the days when the class has gym, art,

   and an hour of math games. _____

   _____

   b) How many times in 100 days does the class have gym, art,

   and an hour of math games? _____

CHAPTER 1

6 Multiple Number Patterns

Goal Extend and describe special number patterns.

1. a) Complete this number chain.

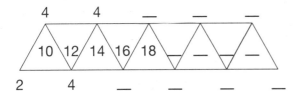

b) Write each number pattern.

inside the triangles:

_____

top corner numbers:

_____

bottom corner numbers:

_____

zig-zag numbers:

_____

At-Home Help

This is a **number chain**.

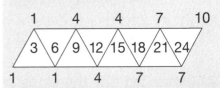

The numbers at the corners of each triangle add to give the number inside the triangle.

1 + 1 + 1 = 3
1 + 1 + 4 = 6

Patterns in this number chain are
inside triangles:
3, 6, 9, 12, 15, 18, 21, 24
top corner numbers:
1, 4, 4, 7, 10
bottom corner numbers:
1, 1, 4, 7, 7
zig-zag numbers:
1, 1, 1, 4, 4, 4, 7, 7, 7, 10

2. Complete this number chain.

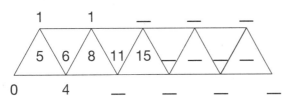

Write each number pattern.

inside the triangles: _____

top corner numbers: _____

bottom corner numbers: _____

zig-zag numbers: _____

6 Chapter 1: Patterns in Mathematics

Copyright © 2004 Nelson

7 Finding Missing Terms

Goal Find the missing number in a pattern and in an equation.

1. Use the equation to find the missing number in each pattern. Then write the pattern rule.

a) _____ + 5 = 28   3, 8, 13, 18, _____, 28, ...

_____

b) _____ + 10 = 45   25, _____, 45, 55, 65, ...

_____

c) _____ + 4 = 23   3, 7, 11, 15, _____, 23, 27, ...

_____

d) _____ + 6 = 51   _____, 51, 57, 63, 69, 75, ...

_____

e) _____ − 4 = 50   _____, 50, 46, 42, 38, 34, ...

_____

f) _____ − 3 = 53   62, 59, _____, 53, 50, 47, ...

_____

2. Fill in the blank in each equation.

a) 5 + _____ = 20   c) 27 + _____ = 31   e) 82 − _____ = 76

b) 23 − _____ = 19   d) _____ + 8 = 34   f) _____ − 9 = 26

8 Equivalent Equations

Goal Use patterns to create equations.

You will need counters, such as toothpicks, bread tags, or dry cereal.

1. You can use counters to find all the number pairs for ● and ■ that make 8 + 3 = ● + ■ true.

$8 + 3 = ● + ■$

●	■
0	11
1	10
2	9
3	8
4	7

   a) Show 8 + 3 using counters.

   b) Rearrange the counters to show the number pairs given in the At-Home Help box.

   c) Keep rearranging the counters to find all the number pairs. ● = 1 and ■ = 10 is a different number pair than ● = 10 and ■ = 1. Continue the pattern and record the other number pairs in this t-chart.

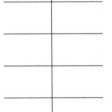

   d) Describe any patterns you see in the t-chart.

   _____

   _____

2. Use a t-chart and patterns to find all the number pairs for ● and ■ that make 5 + 5 = ● + ■ true.

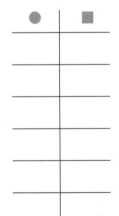

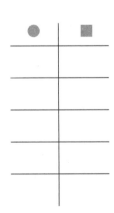

Test Yourself Page 1

Circle the correct answer.

1. Which letter pattern describes this bead pattern?

A.
```
        S
       / \
  R — R   T — T
       \ /
        S
```

C.
```
        S
       / \
  R — R   R — T
       \ /
        S
```

B.
```
        S
       / \
  R — R   U — V
       \ /
        T
```

D.
```
        S
       / \
  R — R   R — U
       \ /
        T
```

2. What are the next 3 numbers in this pattern?
   36, 33, 30, 27, …

   E. 24, 21, 18   **F.** 21, 18, 15   **G.** 30, 33, 36   **H.** 26, 25, 24

3. What is the pattern in the 2nd column of this t-chart?

   A. The numbers increase by 1.

   B. The numbers increase by 2.

   C. The numbers increase by 3.

   D. The numbers double.

Number of bracelets	Total number of charms
1	3
2	6
3	9
4	12
5	15

4. What is the pattern for the black squares?

   E. 2, 4, 6, 8, …   **G.** 1, 3, 5, 7, 9, …

   F. 3, 6, 9, 12, …   **H.** 3, 9, 15, …

Test Yourself Page 2

Circle the correct answer.

5. Sari can make 3 paper flowers in 1 hour.
Which t-chart shows how many flowers she can make
in increasing numbers of hours?

A.

Hours	Total number of flowers
0	1
1	3
2	6
3	9
4	12

C.

Hours	Total number of flowers
0	3
1	6
3	12
4	15

B.

Hours	Total number of flowers
1	3
2	6
3	9
4	12
5	15

D.

Hours	Total number of flowers
1	3
2	3
3	3
4	3
5	3

6. What is the next number in the zig-zag pattern?

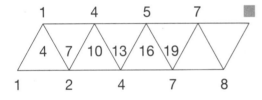

	1	4	5	7	■
	4	7	10	13	16	19
1	2	4	7	8

E. 10   **F.** 25   **G.** 8   **H.** 9

7. What is the missing number in this pattern?
32, 35, ■, 41, 44, 47, ...

A. 36   **B.** 37   **C.** 38   **D.** 39

8. Which of these could be the right side of the equation
$14 + 9 = \bullet + \blacksquare$?

E. 14 + 10   **F.** 13 + 10   **G.** 13 + 9   **H.** 13 + 8

CHAPTER 2

1 Place Value

Goal **Model numbers up to 10 000.**

1. Suppose you used only 1 type of block to
   model each number. How many hundreds
   blocks would you need? How many
   thousands blocks would you need?

   a) 1000 _____ hundreds or _____ thousands

   b) 3000 _____ hundreds or _____ thousands

   c) 8000 _____ hundreds or _____ thousands

2. Write the number for each.

   a) _____

   b) _____

   c) _____

> **At-Home Help**
>
> **Base ten blocks** are often used
> to **model** or represent place
> value concepts.
>
> □   represents one.
>
> ▯   represents ten.
>
> ▢   represents one hundred.
>
> ▣   represents one thousand.
>
> For example, 2465 can be
> modelled as

3. A school collected 2724 cans for the canned food drive by the end
   of November.

   a) Which blocks would you use to model 2724 with the least

      number of blocks? _____

      _____

   b) Imagine that blocks are added to include 100 more cans
      collected each week for 4 weeks. Which blocks would be added?

      _____

   c) Imagine that blocks are traded so the model uses the least number
      of blocks. Which blocks would change? Why?

      _____

      _____

2 Expanded Form

Goal Write numbers up to 10 000 in expanded form.

1.

Thousands	Hundreds	Tens	Ones
2	1	8	4

Write the modelled number

a) in standard form _____

b) in expanded form using numbers

_____

c) in expanded form using words _____

_____

d) as you would read it _____

_____

2. Write each number in expanded form using words.

a) 6734 _____

b) 3208 _____

c) 9777 _____

3. Write each number in standard form.

a)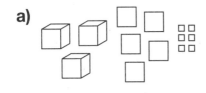

_____

b) 8000 + 800 + 80 + 8 _____

c) 7 thousands + 6 tens + 2 ones _____

3 Comparing and Ordering Numbers

Goal Compare and order numbers up to 10 000.

1. Here are the masses of some heavy animals.

 elephant
6168 kg

 giraffe
1364 kg

 rhinoceros
2273 kg

 baby whale
3636 kg

 bison
1182 kg

 hippopotamus
3207 kg

At–Home Help

When comparing numbers, you can use the symbols < and >. The symbol < means that the 1st number is less than the 2nd number.
The symbol > means that the 1st number is greater than the 2nd number.
The symbols < and > always point to the lesser number (e.g., 1805 < 5920 and 5920 > 1805).

a) Which animal is the heaviest? Explain how you know. _____

_____

b) Which animals have a mass of between 2000 kg and 4000 kg? _____

_____

c) Which animal is heavier, the giraffe or the bison? Explain how you know.

_____

_____

d) Order the animals from lightest to heaviest. _____

_____

2. Complete by using <, =, or >.

   a) 8882 ___ 987   b) 2815 ___ 2968   c) 6200 ___ 8602   d) 5432 ___ 4523

3. Write each set of numbers in order from least to greatest.

   a) 7450, 6871, 7531, 784 _____

   b) 5871, 5873, 5997, 5888 _____

4 Exploring 10 000

Goal Explore place value patterns to 10 000.

1. Write the first 5 numbers in each pattern.

   a) The pattern starts with 6 thousands.
   The number of thousands increases by
   1 for each number.

   _____

   _____

   b) The pattern starts with 9 thousands + 9 hundreds + 8 tens.
   The number of ones increases by 5 for each number.

   _____

   c) The pattern starts with 9 thousands + 9 hundreds + 2 tens.
   The number of tens increases by 2 for each number.

   _____

   d) The pattern starts with 9 thousands + 2 hundreds.
   The number of hundreds increases by 2 for each number.

   _____

2. Complete each pattern by filling in the missing numbers.

   a) 5000, 6000, _____, 8000, 9000, _____

   b) 2000, 4000, _____, _____, 10 000

   c) 9960, _____, 9980, 9990, _____

   d) 9750, 9800, 9850, _____, 9950, _____

   e) 9995, 9996, _____, 9998, _____, _____

   f) 9990, 9992, 9994, 9996, _____, _____

CHAPTER 2

5   Multiplying by 10, 100, and 1000

Goal   Multiply by 10, 100, and 1000.

1. Multiply.

     a) 7 × 10 = _____   **c)** 50 × 10 = _____

     b) 29 × 10 = _____   **d)** 321 × 10 = _____

2. What pattern do you see in your answers to

     Question 1? _____

     _____

> **At-Home Help**
>
> When you multiply 3, for example, by 10, you have 3 groups of 10.
>
> There are 3 tens and 0 ones. So 3 × 10 = 30.

3. Multiply.

     a) 5 × 100 = _____   **c)** 70 × 100 = _____

     b) 38 × 100 = _____   **d)** 100 × 100 = _____

4. What pattern do you see in your answers to Question 3? _____

     _____

5. Multiply.

     a) 2 × 1000 = _____   **c)** 9 × 1000 = _____

     b) 5 × 1000 = _____   **d)** 10 × 1000 = _____

6. What pattern do you see in your answers to Question 5? _____

     _____

7. What is the missing number?

     a) 3000 = _____ × 1000   **c)** 6000 = _____ × 1000

     b) 3000 = _____ × 100   **d)** 6000 = _____ × 100

8. What is the missing number?

     a) 4290 = _____ × 10   **c)** 7500 = _____ × 10

     b) 3060 = _____ × 10   **d)** 9000 = _____ × 10

CHAPTER 2

6

Rounding to the Nearest 10, 100, or 1000

Goal Round numbers to the nearest 10, 100, or 1000.

1. There are 4906 grade 4 students in the Ottawa-Carleton school district. Round this number to

   a) the nearest thousand _____

   b) the nearest hundred _____

   c) the nearest ten _____

2. a) Draw a number line to show how you would round the greatest depth of the Atlantic Ocean to the nearest thousand.

Ocean/Sea	Greatest depth (m)
Indian Ocean	7455
Atlantic Ocean	9219
Arctic Ocean	5625
Caribbean Sea	6946

At-Home Help

There are times when it is useful to use approximate numbers. One way to do this is to **round** numbers to the nearest 10, 100, or 1000. To do this, find the multiple of 10, 100, or 1000 that the number is closest to.

2462 rounded to the nearest thousand is 2000.
2462 rounded to the nearest hundred is 2500.
2465 rounded to the nearest ten is 2470.

b) What is the greatest depth of the Indian Ocean rounded to the nearest thousand? _____

c) What is the greatest depth of the Indian Ocean rounded to the nearest hundred? _____

d) What is the greatest depth of the Arctic Ocean rounded to the nearest thousand? _____

e) What is the greatest depth of the Arctic Ocean rounded to the nearest hundred? _____

f) Explain why the greatest depths of the Caribbean Sea and the Indian Ocean are both 7000 m when rounded to the nearest thousand.

_____

_____

16 Chapter 2: Numeration

Copyright © 2004 Nelson

Communicate About Ordering Numbers

Goal **Explain how to order a set of numbers in a complete, clear, and organized way.**

1. Match the letters of the explanations in the boxes below to these number patterns. If you correctly match the patterns to their explanations, the letters going down will spell the number of patterns you matched.

   a) 8808, 8008, 888, 808 _____

   b) 180, 295, 592, 801 _____

   c) 1000, 5308, 5803, 8500 _____

   d) 8, 81, 808, 8808 _____

At-Home Help

The following terms help describe how a set of numbers is ordered.

digits: The digits in our number system are 0, 1, 2, 3, 4, 5, 6, 7, 8, and 9.

numbers: Combinations of the digits are numbers (e.g., 43, 895, and 2067).

place value: A digit takes on a value determined by the place it occupies in a number.
In the number 4**5**, the digit 5 is in the ones place. Its value is 5. In the number 2**5**1, the digit 5 is in the tens place. Its value is 50. In **5**30, the 5 is in the hundreds place. Its value is 500. In **5**296, the 5 is in the thousands place. Its value is 5000.

R I ordered the numbers from least to greatest with the 1-digit number first, then the 2-digit number, then the 3-digit number, and finally the 4-digit number.

F I ordered the numbers from greatest to least. The first 2 numbers have 4 digits. I compared their hundreds digits to decide which number is greater. The last 2 numbers have 3 digits. I compared their tens digits to decide which number is greater.

U I looked at the digit in the thousands place and wrote the numbers from least to greatest. For the 2 numbers that have the same thousands digit, I looked at the digit in the hundreds place to decide which is the least.

O All of the numbers have 3 digits. I ordered the numbers from least to greatest by looking at the digit in the hundreds place.

8 Counting Money Collections

Goal Estimate, count, and write money amounts up to $50.00.

1. a) Estimate how much money Hannah has.

_____

b) Find the actual amount.

2. Describe bills and coins to make $5.00 in 3 different ways.

way 1: _____

way 2: _____

way 3: _____

3. Hong has 1 twenty-dollar bill, 1 five-dollar bill, 8 quarters, 8 dimes, 1 nickel, and 4 pennies.

a) Estimate the total amount of money he has. _____

b) Find the actual total.

4. How would you make $22.35 using the fewest bills and coins?

Test Yourself

Circle the correct answer.

1. Write the number for these base ten blocks.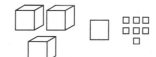

   A. 317   **C.** 3107

   B. 3170   **D.** 3017

2. Write 8945 in expanded form.

   E. 8000 + 900 + 40 + 5   **G.** 8 + 9 + 4 + 5

   F. 8000 + 9000 + 400 + 5   **H.** 89 + 45

3. My thousands digit is 1 more than my hundreds digit.
   The sum of my thousands digit and hundreds digit is 3.
   My thousands digit is the same as my ones digit.
   My hundreds digit is the same as my tens digit.
   What number am I?

   A. 3003   **B.** 3030   **C.** 2121   **D.** 2112

4. Complete by choosing the correct number: 2365 > ■

   E. 2425   **F.** 6523   **G.** 1365   **H.** 2565

5. Multiply: 1000 × 10 = ■

   A. 1000   **B.** 100   **C.** 10 000   **D.** 100 000

6. There are 365 days in 1 year. How many days are in 10 years?

   E. 365   **F.** 3650   **G.** 10 000   **H.** 36 500

7. What number is 1928 rounded to the nearest hundred?

   A. 100   **B.** 1930   **C.** 2000   **D.** 1900

8. Find the total amount for 1 twenty-dollar bill, 1 ten-dollar bill,
   1 five-dollar bill, 3 quarters, 1 dime, and 1 nickel.

   E. $36.15   **F.** $30.90   **G.** $35.95   **H.** $35.90

9. There are 20 quarters, 5 dimes, 5 nickels, and 5 pennies in a jar.
   How much money is in the jar?

   A. $5.80   **B.** $50.80   **C.** $6.80   **D.** $5.25

CHAPTER 3
1 Constructing a Pictograph

Goal **Construct and interpret pictographs.**

1. The chart shows some data for you to display in a pictograph.

At–Home Help

A **pictograph** uses symbols to represent a number of items. For data where the least number of items is 2 and the greatest is 10, the scale could be "Each symbol means 1 item." For data where the least number of items is 20 and the greatest number is 240, the scale could be "Each symbol means 20 items."

Bones Collected

Month	Number of bones
June	25
July	50
August	35
September	15

a) What symbol will you use to represent the

number of bones? _____

b) How many bones will each symbol represent? _____

c) Make the pictograph. Include the title and the scale.

_____

June	
July	
August	
September	
	Scale:

2. a) The spinner landed on the spotted section 24 times.
Fill in the scale to tell what each circle means.

b) How many times did the spinner land
on each of the other sections?

white _____

black _____

grey _____

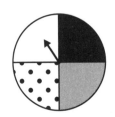

Number of Times Landed On

white ◯ ◯ ◖

black ◯ ◯ ◯ ◖

grey ◯ ◯

spotted ◯ ◯ ◯ ◯

Each ◯ means ___ times.

20 Chapter 3: Data Management

Copyright © 2004 Nelson

CHAPTER 3
2 Choosing a Scale for a Bar Graph

Goal Explain how to choose a graph and a scale that are appropriate for the data.

1. Some students voted on their favourite day of the school week. Complete the bar graph. Choose an appropriate scale and include a title.

> **At-Home Help**
>
> A **bar graph** uses horizontal or vertical bars to show data. For data where the least number of items is 5 and the greatest is 70, the scale could be each grid line represents 10. Then you would need 7 grid lines to get to 70.

Monday

Tuesday

Day Wednesday

Thursday

Friday

Number of students

Day	Number of students
Monday	60
Tuesday	40
Wednesday	25
Thursday	85
Friday	110

2. The hair colour of some grade 4 students is shown. Complete the bar graph. Choose an appropriate scale and include a title.

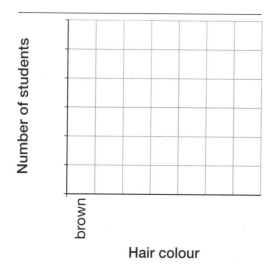

Number of students

brown

Hair colour

Hair colour	Number of students
brown	25
red	5
blond	15
black	10

Copyright © 2004 Nelson

3 Collecting Data

Goal Predict results, collect and organize data, and find the range.

1. Look at the 2 sentences in the At-Home Help box.

   a) Predict the number of times that each letter listed in the chart is used in the 2 sentences. Record your prediction in the 2nd column of the chart.

   b) Count and record the actual number of times each letter is used.
   Record your count in the 3rd column of the chart.

Letter	Prediction of times each letter is used	Count of times each letter is used
a		
e		
i		
o		
u		
c		
k		
s		
t		

2. **a)** Which letter was used the least number of times? _____

   How many times was it used? _____

   b) Which letter was used the greatest number of times? _____

   How many times was it used? _____

   c) What is the range of the counted data? _____

3. Compare your predictions with what you counted. For which letters

   were you close? Why might that be? _____

   _____

CHAPTER 3
4

Constructing a Bar Graph with Intervals

Goal Construct a bar graph using appropriate intervals for the range of data.

1. This chart shows data in intervals. Use it to answer the questions.

Hours of computer time used in 1 month	Number of students
1–10	1
11–20	4
21–30	7
31–40	8
41–50	10

At-Home Help

The chart in Question 1 has 5 **intervals**. Intervals for a set of data should always be equal. In this chart, each interval is 10.

a) What is the least number of hours that could have been used? _____

b) What is the greatest number of hours that could have been used? _____

c) How many students were asked? _____

d) Suppose you wanted to show the number of students in each interval

on a bar graph. How many bars would you need? _____

2. The list on the right shows how many blocks 30 students were able to stack before their stacks fell over.

Number of Blocks in a Stack

6	7	8	9	10
10	11	11	12	12
13	14	14	16	16
17	18	18	18	19
19	19	20	20	21
22	23	23	24	24

a) Complete the chart to show the data in intervals.

Number of blocks stacked before falling	Number of students
1–10	

b) Complete the bar graph on the right using the data from the chart.

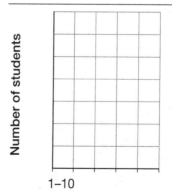

Number of students

1–10

Number of blocks stacked before falling

CHAPTER 3

5 Reading and Interpreting Graphs

Goal Read and interpret graphs and identify their features.

1. Use the pictograph to answer these questions.

At-Home Help

The scale in Question 1 is often called a **legend**. The explanation of colours, such as in Question 3, is also called a **legend**.

Boxes of Food Collected for Charity

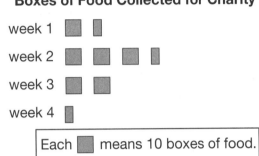

Each ▪ means 10 boxes of food.

a) How many boxes were collected in week 2? _____

b) In which week were the fewest boxes collected? _____

c) How many more boxes were collected in week 2 than in week 4? _____

d) How many boxes were collected altogether? _____

2. Use the bar graph to answer the questions.

a) Which type of ball was the best seller? _____

b) What is the range of these data? _____

c) How many tennis balls were sold? _____

d) How many balls were sold altogether? _____

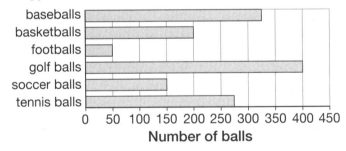

Types of Balls Sold in a Year by a Sports Store

Number of balls

3. Lily says that this circle graph shows that 11 students in a class wear glasses and 21 do not. Do you agree? Explain your thinking. _____

_____

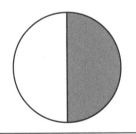

☐ wears glasses
▪ doesn't wear glasses

24 Chapter 3: Data Management

Copyright © 2004 Nelson

6 Graphing with Technology

Goal Use spreadsheet software to organize and display data.

If you have spreadsheet software at home, answer Question 1 to show what you learned about graphing today.

1. Students counted the vehicles passing through an intersection for 5 minutes. The data that they collected were entered into a spreadsheet.

	A	B
1	cars	18
2	vans	13
3	sport utility vehicles	11
4	trucks	9

   a) Enter these data into a spreadsheet.

   b) Make a circle or pie graph of the data.

   c) Why is a legend important? _____

   _____

   d) Change the number of cars to 40. What happens to the graph?

   _____

If you don't have spreadsheet software at home, answer Question 2 to show what you learned about graphing today.

2. Students counted the vehicles passing through an intersection for 5 minutes. The data that they collected were entered into a spreadsheet.

	A	B
1	cars	18
2	vans	13
3	sport utility vehicles	11
4	trucks	9

   a) If these data were displayed in a circle graph, which section would be the largest? _____ Which section would be the smallest? _____

   b) Recall the graphs you made in class. Why is a legend important?

   _____

   c) Recall the graphs you made in class. What would happen to the graph if the number of cars changed to 40? _____

   _____

7 Communicate About Collecting Data

Goal Describe the steps for collecting data in a clear and organized way.

1. Pedro wanted to know what the students in his class want to be when they grow up. Label the steps from 1 to 5 in the order that he did them.

☐ He made a bar graph of his information.

☐ He organized the data he collected in a chart.

☐ He collected the answered survey questions.

☐ He made up a survey question.

☐ He gave each student in his class the survey question and asked them to answer it.

2. Sharleen wanted to know how students travel to school. Label the steps from 1 to 8 in the order that she did them.

☐ She entered the data into spreadsheet software.

☐ She made up a survey question listing the different ways she observed.

☐ She asked the teacher if she could write the question on the board and survey the class.

☐ She read the question that she wrote on the board.

☐ She read the question again and counted how many hands were raised for each way.

☐ She observed students arriving at school to see how they get there.

☐ She graphed these data using the spreadsheet software.

☐ She told the class that she would read the question again, and asked them to raise their hands when she named the way that they usually come to school.

8 Conducting a Survey

Goal **Conduct a survey and make a graph to display the data.**

1. Choose a topic to collect data about.
    - favourite TV show
    - favourite flavour of ice cream
    - favourite hockey team
    - favourite season

At-Home Help

The data from Question 1 can be graphed using any of the types of graphs that you have learned about. After you make your graph, think about why you chose that type of graph.

2. Make up a question. It should have 4 or more choices. Decide if one choice should be "other." Write the question here and write the choices in the 1st column of the chart below.

3. Ask your question to as many people as you can. Ask everyone at home and maybe call some people. Use this chart to organize the results.

Answer chosen	Number of people

4. Make a graph of your findings. Use the grid below or spreadsheet software.

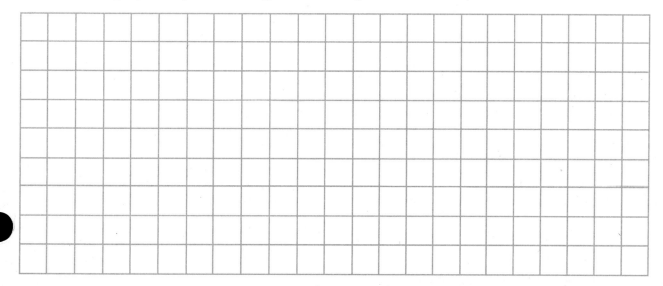

Test Yourself Page 1

Circle the correct answer.

Use this pictograph to answer Questions 1 to 3.

Number of Books Sarah Read

June   📖 📖 📖 📖 📖 📖 📖 📖 📖

July   📖 📖 📖 📖 📖 📖 📖 📖 📖 📖 📖 📖 📖

August   📖 📖 📖 📖 📖 📖 📖 📖 📖 📖 📖 📖

> Each 📖 means 2 books read.

1. How many books did Sarah read in July?

   A. 13   **B.** $8\frac{1}{2}$ **C.** 26   **D.** $11\frac{1}{2}$

2. Sarah wants to add September's reading to her pictograph. She will use $9\frac{1}{2}$ 📖 . How many books did she read in September?

   E. $9\frac{1}{2}$ **F.** 19   **G.** 18   **H.** 20

3. Suppose that the legend or scale was changed to "Each 📖 means 4 books." How would 1 book read be shown?

   A. 📖   **B.** 📖 📖 📖 📖   **C.** 📖   **D.** ▫

Use these data to answer Questions 4 and 5.

17	18	20	20	23
25	26	29	33	34
34	37	39	40	40

4. What is the range of these data?

   E. 23   **F.** 15   **G.** 40   **H.** 17

5. How many pieces of data are in the interval 25–34?

   A. 3   **B.** 4   **C.** 5   **D.** 6

Test Yourself Page 2

Circle the correct answer.

Use this bar graph to answer Questions 6 to 9.

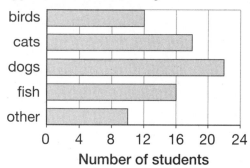

Type of Pets Owned by Grade 4 Students

Number of students

6. Which type of pet is most common?

   E. birds   **F.** cats   **G.** dogs   **H.** fish

7. How many students have fish as pets?

   A. 4   **B.** 16   **C.** 20   **D.** 15

8. How many more students have dogs than cats?

   E. 1   **F.** 2   **G.** 3   **H.** 4

9. If the scale were 2 at the first grid line, instead of 4, which statement would be true?

   A. The last grid line would be 48 instead of 24.

   B. The graph would have to be longer to show the same data.

   C. The graph could be shorter to show the same data.

   D. The last grid line would be 20 instead of 24.

10. The number of people in this interval is 70. What is the scale?

    E. 20, 40, 60, 80

    F. 15, 30, 45, 60   20–29

    G. 10, 20, 30, 40   0

    H. 1, 2, 3, 4

1 Adding Mentally

Goal Use mental math strategies to add 2-digit numbers.

1. Move counters to make the addition easier. Then write the answer.

18 + 9 = _____

2. Use mental addition.

a) 20 + 30 = _____

b) 50 + 20 = _____

c) 19 + 31 = _____

d) 18 + 32 = _____

e) 49 + 21 = _____

At–Home Help

Moving counters from one group to another can sometimes make adding easier.

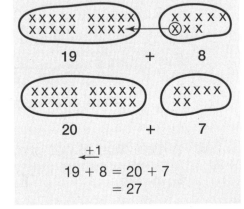

19 + 8 = 20 + 7
= 27

3. Use mental math to solve these problems.

a) There are 38 students in Mrs. Jones's classroom and 23 students in Mr. Singh's classroom.

How many students are there altogether? _____

b) Payden has 48 cents and Jill has 22 cents.

How much money do they have altogether? _____

c) Avis is 19. Her grandmother is 58 years older.

How old is Avis's grandmother? _____

d) There are 37 cans on one shelf and 43 on another.

How many cans are there altogether? _____

e) There are 28 large paper clips and 38 small paper clips.

How many paper clips are there altogether? _____

2 Estimating Sums

Goal **Estimate sums by rounding.**

1. Estimate. Show your rounded numbers.

   a) 1867 + 913 is about equal to

   _____

   b) 3611 + 1489 is about equal to

   _____

   c) 1156 + 2722 is about equal to

   _____

   d) 999 + 1999 is about equal to

   _____

> ### At-Home Help
>
> You can use **rounded numbers** to **estimate a sum** (the answer when you add).
>
> $$3859 + 1321$$
>
> close to 4000   close to 1000
>
> The sum is about
> 4000 + 1000 = 5000.

2. Estimate the answers to these problems. Show your rounded numbers.

   a) Jack's mother drove 1245 km on Saturday and 985 km on Sunday. About how many kilometres did she drive on those 2 days?

   b) 4856 people live in one town. 3345 live in another town. About how many people live in the 2 towns?

   c) 3756 DVDs were rented one week. 4103 DVDs were rented the next week. About how many DVDs were rented those 2 weeks?

3. Use rounded numbers to find whether $5000 is enough to buy both items in each part. Check your answers using a calculator.

   a)

   b)

3 Communicate About Number Concepts and Procedures

Goal Explain your thinking when estimating a sum.

1. Is each answer reasonable? Explain.

   a) 1899 + 976 = 2875 _____

   _____

   b) 4521 + 2589 = 7110 _____

   _____

   c) 3464 + 1987 = 7451 _____

   _____

   d) 1569 + 3750 = 4319 _____

   _____

   e) 3122 + 3179 = 6301 _____

   _____

At-Home Help

Estimation can help you to find out if an answer is **reasonable**.

6 3 3 2

This answer to 2567 + 3765 is reasonable because 2000 + 3000 = 5000 and 3000 + 4000 = 7000. The answer should be between 5000 and 7000.

---

2. Use a calculator to solve each problem.
   Explain why your answer is reasonable.

   a) 1517 tickets were sold for blue seats at a hockey game.
   3567 tickets were sold for red seats.
   How many tickets were sold altogether? _____

   _____

   b) 5245 children's tickets were sold for a circus.
   2345 adult tickets were sold.
   How many tickets were sold altogether? _____

   _____

4 Adding 4-Digit Numbers

Goal **Solve addition problems using regrouping.**

1. Complete the addition by writing in the spaces in the place value chart.

At-Home Help

You can add two 4-digit numbers by **regrouping**.

2539 + 1866

a)

Thousands	Hundreds	Tens	Ones
		1	
2	7	3	2
2	8	6	9
			1

Thousands	Hundreds	Tens	Ones
1	1	1	
2	5	3	9
1	8	6	6
4	4	0	5

```
  1 1 1
   2539
 + 1866
 ------
   4405
```

b)

Thousands	Hundreds	Tens	Ones
2	7	3	8
6	4	3	9
		7	

The answer seems reasonable because 3000 + 2000 = 5000 and the answer is close to 5000.

2. Estimate the sum. Then add.

a) 3988
   + 2246

b) 3254
   + 862

c) 4310
   + 3859

3. Estimate. Then solve.

a) There are 3456 Girl Guides in one area and 1672 in another area. What is the total number of Girl Guides in both areas?

b) There are 1867 Wolf Cubs in one area and 4306 in another area. What is the total number of Wolf Cubs in both areas?

5 Subtracting Mentally

Goal **Develop mental math strategies for subtracting 2-digit numbers.**

1. Add the same number to each number to make subtracting easier. Record only the answer.

   a) 56 − 18 = _____

   b) 61 − 19 = _____

   c) 45 − 28 = _____

   d) 51 − 39 = _____

   e) 32 − 9 = _____

   f) 75 − 49 = _____

   g) 83 − 28 = _____

   h) 65 − 48 = _____

At-Home Help

Adding the same number to each number in a subtraction question does not change the answer.

$$6 + 2 \longrightarrow 8$$
$$\underline{-1 + 2} \longrightarrow \underline{-3}$$
$$5 \qquad\qquad 5$$

Adding the same number can sometimes make it easier to subtract.

$$37 + 2 \longrightarrow 39$$
$$\underline{-18 + 2} \longrightarrow \underline{-20}$$
$$19$$

$$37 − 18 = 39 − 20$$
$$= 19$$

2. Use mental math to solve each problem.

   a) It is 33°C in one town and 9°C in another town.
   What is the difference in temperature between the towns?

   _____

   b) Licorice costs 62 cents. Gumballs cost 39 cents.
   How much more does the licorice cost than the gumballs?

   _____

   c) 19 cm is cut from a 51 cm ribbon.
   How many centimetres long is the ribbon now?

   _____

   d) There are 71 students in grade 4.
   39 are girls. How many students are boys?

   _____

6 Estimating Differences

Goal **Estimate differences by rounding.**

1. Estimate. Show your rounded numbers.

   a) 2867 − 913 is about equal to

   _____

   b) 4511 − 1489 is about equal to

   _____

   c) 6156 − 722 is about equal to

   _____

   d) 4999 − 1099 is about equal to _____

   e) 8504 − 2571 is about equal to _____

At-Home Help

You can use rounded numbers to **estimate a difference** (the answer when you subtract).

4859 − 2598

close to 5000   close to 2500

The difference is about 5000 − 2500 = 2500.

2. Estimate the answers to these problems. Show your rounded numbers.

   a) A library has 6756 books. 2567 are on loan. About how many books are left in the library?

   _____

   b) A plane flying at a height of 7458 m drops down 3288 m. At about what height is it flying now?

   _____

   c) Mount Logan, the highest point in Canada, is 5959 m tall. Mount Everest, the highest point in the world, is 8850 m tall. About how much taller is Mount Everest than Mount Logan?

   _____

3. Estimate to show if the answer is reasonable.

   7653 − 2987 = 2666 _____

CHAPTER 4

7 Subtracting from 4-Digit Numbers

Goal Use a paper and pencil method to subtract from a 4-digit number.

1. Estimate the difference. Then subtract. Show your work.

a) 3234
   − 533

d) 8129
   − 411

b) 2045
   − 1236

e) 1566
   − 807

c) 2000
   − 621

f) 5003
   − 347

At-Home Help

You can subtract larger numbers by regrouping the top number in several steps.

```
   013516
   1̶3̶6̶6̶
 −  448
 ─────
    918
```

The answer seems reasonable because 1400 − 400 = 1000 and 918 is close to 1000.

2. Estimate and solve.

a) The average yearly precipitation (rain and snow) in Toronto is 819 mm. The greatest average yearly precipitation in Canada is 6655 mm in Henderson Lake, B.C. What is the difference in precipitation between Henderson Lake and Toronto?

b) A town has 1100 adults. 589 are women. How many men are there?

c) A school is trying to raise $1000 for a charity. $795 has already been raised. How much more money must the school raise?

36 Chapter 4: Addition and Subtraction

Copyright © 2004 Nelson

8 Subtracting in a Different Way

Goal Use regrouping to make subtraction easier.

1. Finish each subtraction.

a)
```
   1 9 9 9 + 1
   2̶0̶0̶0̶
 −  655
```

b)
```
   2 9 9 9 + 4
   3̶0̶0̶3̶
 −  635
```

c)
```
   4 9 9 9 + 2
   5̶0̶0̶1̶
 − 1872
```

At-Home Help

If the top number in a subtraction has many zeroes, you can regroup in 1 step.

```
    1 9 9 9  + 1
    2̶0̶0̶0̶    |
  −  755     ↓
    1244 + 1 = 1245
```

The answer is reasonable because 2000 − 800 = 1200 and 1245 is close to 1200.

2. Estimate each difference. Then subtract. Show your work.

a)
```
   3000
 −  533
```

c)
```
   2005
 −  621
```

e)
```
   1000
 −  807
```

b)
```
   2000
 − 1236
```

d)
```
   8000
 −  411
```

f)
```
   5003
 − 1347
```

3. Correct any unreasonable answers.

a) 8000 − 178 = 7822

b) 3000 − 488 = 2812

9 Making Change

Goal Make purchases and change for money amounts.

1. Finish the steps to find the change.

a) $1.55

$1.55 + **5 cents** = $1.60

$1.60 + _____ = $2.00

The change is _____.

b) $3.48

$3.48 + **2 cents** = $3.50

$3.50 + _____ = $4.00

$4.00 + _____ = $10.00

The change is _____.

At-Home Help

You can **count on from a price** to determine the amount of change after buying something.

The item costs $12.35 and you have a $20 bill.

$12.35 + **5 cents** = $12.40
$12.40 + **60 cents** = $13.00
$13.00 + **$7.00** = $20.00

The change is $7.00 + 60 cents + 5 cents = $7.65.

---

2. Find the change.

a) $12.75

b) $23.95

c) $36.98

d) $42.50

10 Adding and Subtracting Money

Goal Use different methods to add and subtract money.

1. Add or subtract one way.
   Use another way to check your answer.

   a) $10.99 + $15.67

   b) $30.00 − $16.95

   c) $4.99 + $4.99

   d) $15.00 − $9.98

   e) $14.25 + $5.75

   f) $20.00 − $14.25

At-Home Help

There are many ways to add and subtract prices ending in 98 or 99.

To add $9.99 and $8.56,
take 1¢ from $8.56,
add 1¢ to $9.99,
and add the new amounts.
  $9.99 + $8.56
$10.00 + $8.55 = $18.55

Or to add $9.99 and $8.56, add 1¢ to $9.99 to get $10, add $10.00 and $8.56, and subtract 1¢ from the total.

  $9.99 + $8.56
$10.00 + $8.56 = $18.56
$18.56 −1¢ = $18.55

To subtract $9.99 from $20, add 1¢ to each amount, and subtract the new amounts.

$20.00 − $9.99
$20.01 − $10.00 = $10.01

Or to subtract $9.99 from $20, add 1¢ to $9.99 to get $10, subtract $10.00 from $20.00, and add 1¢ to the answer.
$20.00 − $9.99
$20.00 − $10.00 = $10.00
$10.00 +1¢ = $10.01

2. Find the total cost of the items.
   Then find the change from $10.00.

Chapter 4: Addition and Subtraction **39**

Test Yourself

Circle the correct answer.

1. Use mental math to find which answer is equal to 21.

   A. 69 − 40   **B.** 45 − 26   **C.** 70 − 49   **D.** 50 − 38

2. Use estimation to find which answer is greater than 2000.

   E. 2988 − 1875   **F.** 7345 − 5988   **G.** 998 + 869   **H.** 6134 − 3978

3. Which answer is equal to 4567 + 2366?

   A. 2188 + 4114   **B.** 2620 + 3373   **C.** 5065 + 937   **D.** 4829 + 2104

4. Which answer is equal to 481?

   E. 1050 − 669   **F.** 1300 − 809   **G.** 1230 − 649   **H.** 1000 − 519

5. There are 3456 people watching a parade on one side
   of a street and 2859 watching on the other side.
   How many people are watching the parade?

   A. 5315   **B.** 4315   **C.** 6315   **D.** 597

6. One plane is flying at a height of 5000 m.
   Another plane is flying at a height of 599 m.
   What is the difference in height between the planes?

   E. 4403 m   **F.** 4401 m   **G.** 3401 m   **H.** 5599 m

7. A DVD costs $19.95 and a book costs $8.95.
   How much less than $40 is the total cost of the items?

   A. $11.10   **B.** $10.10   **C.** $12.10   **D.** $28.90

8. Which pair of items costs the most?

   E.    **G.**

   F.    **H.**

1 Measuring with Decimetres

Goal Measure with decimetres and relate decimetres
to centimetres and metres.

You will need a metric ruler.

1. Many measurements begin with estimates.
   People often use reference lengths to help
   them estimate. Find something around your
   home that is about 1 dm long or wide or tall.
   Complete this statement.

> **At-Home Help**
>
> A **decimetre** is a unit of length
> that is between a centimetre
> and a metre.
>
> 1 dm = 10 cm
> 10 dm = 1 m

_____ is about 1 dm _____.

2. Use your object from Question 1. Is the length of each item
   longer or shorter than 1 dm?

   a) a new pencil _____

   b) an eraser _____

   c) a pop can _____

   d) your thumb _____

   e) a remote control _____

   f) a loaf of bread _____

   g) a spoon _____

   h) a toothpick _____

3. a) Draw a line that you think is 1 dm long using a straight edge
      that is not a ruler.

   b) Use a ruler to measure your estimated line.
      Correct the line to make it exactly 1 dm.

   c) Was your estimate shorter or longer than the measured line?

      By how much? _____

   d) How many centimetres long is your measured line? _____

4. Find and name 2 objects at home that would be better measured in

   decimetres than metres._____

   _____

2 Measuring with Millimetres

Goal Use millimetres to measure with precision.

You will need a ruler marked in millimetres.

1. Give an estimate in millimetres. Then measure the object to check your estimate.

   a) the thickness of a penny

   estimate: _____

   measure: _____

   b) the greatest distance across a penny

   estimate: _____

   measure: _____

   c) the width of your baby finger

   estimate: _____   measure: _____

   d) the thickness of a shelf

   estimate: _____   measure: _____

2. Look at this line. ━━━━━━━━

   a) Estimate how many millimetres you would have to add to

   make the line 1 dm long. _____

   b) Measure to check your estimate. How close were you?

   _____

3. The length of a fork is about 2 dm.

   a) What is its length in centimetres? _____

   b) What is its length in millimetres? _____

At-Home Help

A **millimetre** is a unit of measurement that is shorter than a centimetre.

10 mm = 1 cm

1 mm   10 mm or 1 cm

The space between the small markings is 1 mm.

The space from 20 mm to 30 mm is 10 mm, or 1 cm.

Smaller units allow you to measure more precisely.

CHAPTER 5
3
Record Measures Using Multiple Units

Goal Measure and record using a combination of units.

You will need a ruler marked in millimetres.

1. Which measurement is more precise?

   a) 4 m or 3 m 97 cm _____

   b) 104 mm or 10 cm _____

2. Complete.

   a) 246 cm = 2 m _____ cm

   b) 44 mm = _____ cm 4 mm

   c) 165 mm = 16 cm _____ mm

   d) 4 m 16 cm = _____ cm

   e) 7 cm 4 mm = _____ mm

   f) 17 cm 3 mm = _____ mm

3. Use a ruler to draw each line.

   a) 13 cm

   b) 8 cm 4 mm

   c) 73 mm

4. Complete.

   a) 31 mm = _____ cm _____ mm

   b) 47 mm = _____ cm _____ mm

   c) 2500 m – _____ km _____ m

   d) 45 cm = _____ dm _____ cm

At-Home Help

Measurements sometimes include 2 units. Large units use smaller numbers and are easier to picture. Using smaller units makes the measurement more precise.

It is important to state the units when measuring. Without units, the numbers have no meaning.

This line is 26 mm or 2 cm 6 mm.

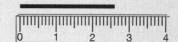

4 Solve Problems by Drawing Diagrams

Goal Use diagrams to solve problems.

You will need a ruler.

1. Alyssa lives 28 km north of Ben.
   Kara lives 13 km south of Ben.
   How far apart do Alyssa and Kara live?

2. Ming is flying a kite. At first the kite flies 12 m
   above him. Then he lets out more string and
   the kite goes up another 3 m. The wind dies
   down and the kite sinks 5 m. As the wind
   picks up, the kite goes 7 m higher.
   How many metres above Ming is the kite now?

At-Home Help

A diagram helps when solving
some problems.

On a hiking trail, a sign says
Lookout A is 2 km west and
Lookout B is 500 m east. What
is the distance from the sign to
Lookout A, then to Lookout B,
and back to the sign?

2 km ←
2 km →

500 m →
500 m ←

$4 \text{ km} + 1000 \text{ m} = 4 \text{ km} + 1 \text{ km}$
$= 5 \text{ km}$

3. Ethan walked 3 blocks north, 2 blocks west, 5 blocks south,
   3 blocks east, and 2 blocks north. How many blocks is Ethan
   from his starting point? Is he north, south, east, or west
   of his starting point?

5 Perimeter of Rectangles

Goal Use the length and width of a rectangle to find its perimeter.

You will need a metric ruler.

1. a) Use the given length and width to find the perimeter of the rectangle.

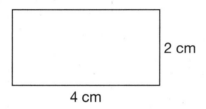

2 cm

4 cm

b) Measure the distance around the rectangle to check.

2. Calculate the perimeter of each rectangle.

a) 14 cm long and 12 cm wide

b) 20 m long and 9 m wide

c) 56 cm long and 13 cm wide

At-Home Help

The **perimeter** of a shape is the distance around the shape.

The perimeter of this rectangle is
3 m + 5 m + 3 m + 5 m = 16 m.

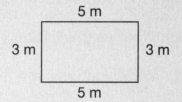

5 m

3 m   3 m

5 m

Because opposite sides are the same length, you can add 2 adjacent sides (a length and a width) and double the sum to find the perimeter.

The perimeter of this rectangle is
double (4 m + 6 m) = double (10 m)
= 20 m

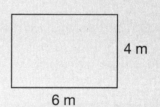

4 m

6 m

3. a) A rectangle is 7 cm wide and 9 cm long. What is its perimeter?

b) What happens to the perimeter of the rectangle if the length increases by 2 cm? What is the new perimeter?

6 Decades, Centuries, and Millenniums

Goal Relate decades, centuries, and millenniums.

1. **a)** What year is it now? _____

   b) What year was it 1 decade ago? _____

   c) What year will it be 1 decade from now? _____

   d) What year was it 1 century ago? _____

   e) What year will it be 1 century from now? _____

   f) What year was it 1 millennium ago? _____

   g) What year will it be 1 millennium from now? _____

> **At-Home Help**
>
> Large time intervals have names—decade, century, and millennium.
>
> 1 decade = 10 years
> 1 century = 100 years
> 1 millennium = 1000 years

2. A family has lived in the same house for 22 years.

   a) How many complete decades is that? _____

   b) In how many more years will it be another complete decade? _____

3. Mayfield School was built in 1920. After 1 century, it will celebrate its

   centennial year. What year will that be? _____

4. Express in years.

   a) $\frac{1}{2}$ a century _____

   b) a decade and a $\frac{1}{2}$ _____

   c) 3 centuries _____

5. Fill in the year.

   a) 2 decades before 2010 _____

   b) 3 decades after 2010 _____

   c) the midpoint of this century _____

7 Time in Minutes

Goal **Find out how long an event takes.**

1. Lata went to her friend's house to play on a Saturday afternoon. The clocks show the time when she left and when she returned home.

a) What time did she leave? _____

b) What time did she return? _____

c) How long was she away? _____

2. How long does each event take?

a) walking to school _____

b) watching a movie _____

At-Home Help

This clock shows when Alex arrived at his grandmother's house.

This clock shows when Alex left his grandmother's house.

He was at his grandmother's for 1 hour 25 minutes, or 85 minutes.

From 1:25 to 2:25 is 1 hour, or 60 minutes.
From 2:25 to 2:50 is 25 minutes.
So the total time was 1 hour 25 minutes, or 85 minutes.

3. Bill is playing soccer in his backyard with friends.
They start the game at 4:05 and play for 45 minutes.
Bill needs to be in the house by 5:00. Will he make it? Explain.

Test Yourself

You will need a ruler marked in millimetres.
Circle the correct answer.

1. Which object is shorter than a decimetre?

   A. a metre stick   **B.** an eraser   **C.** a newspaper   **D.** a person

2. Use a ruler. How many millimetres are between 30 mm and 70 mm?

   E. 40 mm   **F.** 4 mm   **G.** 400 mm   **H.** 37 mm

3. What does 323 cm equal?

   A. 3 m 32 cm   **B.** 300 m 23 cm   **C.** 3 m 23 cm   **D.** 32 m 3 cm

4. 2 friends walk 40 m from the parking lot to the beginning of a 3 km
   hiking trail. They realize that they left their water bottles in the car.
   They go back to get their water bottles, then walk the trail, and
   return to the car. How far do they walk in total?

   E. 3 km 40 m   **F.** 3 km 80 m   **G.** 3 km 120 m   **H.** 3 km 160 m

5. What is the perimeter of this rectangle?

   A. 10 cm   **C.** 24 cm

   B. 14 cm   **D.** 7 cm

   5 cm   2 cm

6. What year is 1 century after 2006?

   E. 2106   **F.** 3006   **G.** 2016   **H.** 2026

7. Jesse and Dan went for a canoe ride. How long were they gone?

   start    end

   A. 3 hours 3 minutes   **C.** 3 hours 57 minutes

   B. 3 hours 23 minutes   **D.** 2 hours 57 minutes

1 Using Doubling to Multiply

Goal Use repeated addition and doubling to multiply.

1. a) $3 + 3 + 3 + 3 + 3 + 3 + 3 + 3 =$ _____

b) Skip count by 3s to 24.

_____

c) How many 3s did you count? _____

d) How much is 8×3? _____

e) How much is 8×6? _____

2. Find each product.

a) $2 \times 8 =$ _____   **c)** $5 \times 7 =$ _____   **e)** $3 \times 6 =$ _____

b) $4 \times 8 =$ _____   **d)** $10 \times 7 =$ _____   **f)** $6 \times 6 =$ _____

3. Write a multiplication equation.

a) $8 + 8 + 8 + 8 + 8$ _____

b) four 7s _____

c) $9 + 9 + 9$ _____

d) five 4s _____

4. Use any strategy to find each product.

a) $3 \times 4 =$ _____   **c)** $2 \times 9 =$ _____

b) $6 \times 4 =$ _____   **d)** $4 \times 9 =$ _____

5. a) How many days are in 1 week? _____

b) How many full weeks of summer holidays do you have? _____

c) How many days is the number of weeks in part b)? _____

CHAPTER 6

2 Sharing and Grouping

Goal Use 2 meanings for division to solve problems.

1. Circle the correct answer.

⠿ ⠿ ⠿ shows

A. $12 \div 4 = 3$ **C.** $16 \div 2 = 8$

B. $16 \div 4 = 4$ **D.** $16 \div 8 = 2$

2. Write and solve the division equation.

a) There are 36 bottles with 6 bottles in each box. How many boxes are there?

b) There are 27 plants with 3 plants in each pot. How many pots are there?

c) 8 students share 32 pieces of paper equally. How many pieces does each student get?

> **At-Home Help**
>
> Division can have 2 meanings.
>
> **Sharing**
> When you know the number of groups, you can find how many are in each group's share.
>
> 24 books to be shared among 6 groups:
> $24 \div 6 = 4$
> There are 4 books for each group.
>
> **Grouping**
> When you know each group's share, you can find the number of groups.
>
> 24 books with 4 books to a group:
> $24 \div 4 = 6$
> 6 groups get books.

3. Complete each division equation.

a) $14 \div 7 = $ _____   **c)** $21 \div 3 = $ _____   **e)** $24 \div 3 = $ _____

b) $35 \div 5 = $ _____   **d)** $48 \div 6 = $ _____   **f)** $45 \div 9 = $ _____

4. There are 24 cookies in a box.
Each person gets the same number of cookies.
Each person gets at least 3 cookies.
What is the greatest number of people that can share the cookies?

3 Division and Multiplication

Goal **Relate multiplication to division.**

1. Complete each division equation.
   Then write a related multiplication equation.

   a) $12 \div 3 =$ _____   _____ $\times$ _____ $=$ _____

   b) $21 \div 7 =$ _____   _____

   c) $32 \div 8 =$ _____   _____

   d) $27 \div 3 =$ _____   _____

2. Complete each multiplication equation.
   Then write a related division equation.

   a) $4 \times 5 =$ _____   _____ $\div$ _____ $=$ _____

   b) $3 \times 8 =$ _____   _____

   c) $6 \times 6 =$ _____   _____

   d) $4 \times 7 =$ _____   _____

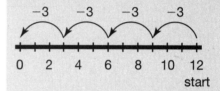
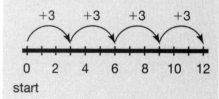

At-Home Help

Multiplication and division are related. Multiplication can be used to check division.

$12 \div 4 = 3$

$4 \times 3 = 12$

start

3. **a)** Write a division equation for the number line. _____

   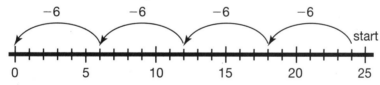

   b) Write a related multiplication equation. _____

4. $12 is shared equally among 4 children. How much money does each child receive? Check your answer by multiplying.

5. Sal earned $25 for working 5 hours. Joe earned $16 for working 4 hours. Who earned the most in an hour? Check your answer by multiplying.

4 Arrays for Fact Families

Goal Describe arrays using fact families.

1. Write the fact family for each array.

   a) X X X X _____ × _____ = _____
   X X X X _____ × _____ = _____
   X X X X _____ ÷ _____ = _____
   _____ ÷ _____ = _____

   b) X X X X X X _____
   X X X X X X _____
   X X X X X X _____
   _____

   c) X X X X X _____
   X X X X X _____
   X X X X X _____
   X X X X X _____

2. Draw an array for each multiplication.
   Then write the product.

   a) 3×8 b) 7×3

3. Use the given fact to write the whole fact family.

   a) $5 \times 6 = 30$ _____ _____ _____

   b) $24 \div 6 = 4$ _____ _____ _____

4. Sometimes a fact family does not have 4 related facts.
   Show an example.

At-Home Help

2 multiplication facts and
2 division facts that describe the
same array are a **fact family**.

X X X X
X X X X

$2 \times 4 = 8$ $8 \div 2 = 4$
$4 \times 2 = 8$ $8 \div 4 = 2$

CHAPTER 6
5 Using Facts to Multiply Larger Numbers

Goal Use basic facts, patterns, and mental math to multiply.

1. Find the products.

   a) 3 × 3 = _____

   b) 3 × 30 = _____

   c) 3 × 300 = _____

   d) 4 × 8 = _____

   e) 4 × 80 = _____

   f) 4 × 800 = _____

   g) 4 × 5 = _____

   h) 4 × 50 = _____

   i) 4 × 500 = _____

   j) 6 × 3 = _____

   k) 6 × 30 = _____

   l) 6 × 300 = _____

2. Find the products.

   a) 2 × 40 = _____

   b) 4 × 20 = _____

   c) 3 × 700 = _____

   d) 3 × 600 = _____

   e) 5 × 8000 = _____

   f) 7 × 3000 = _____

At-Home Help

To find the product of large numbers, use basic facts, patterns in multiplying by 10 and 100, and mental math.

3 × 40 = 120

Think:
   3 × 4 tens
= 12 tens
= 1 hundred 2 tens
= 120

3 × 400 = 1200

Think:
   3 × 4 hundreds
= 12 hundreds
= 1 thousand 2 hundreds
= 1200

3. Circle the correct answer.

   a) 6 × 40 =
   A. 2400   **B.** 24   **C.** 240   **D.** 100

   b) 7 × 500 =
   E. 3500   **F.** 35 000   **G.** 1200   **H.** 350

   c) 5 × 9000 =
   A. 450   **B.** 14 000   **C.** 45 000   **D.** 4500

4. a) How many cans are in 50 boxes? Show your work.

6 cans

   b) How many paper clips are in 7 boxes? Show your wo

300 paper clips

6 Solve Problems by Making Models

Goal **Make models to solve problems.**

You will need 20 toothpicks, 20 buttons, or any 20 small objects of the same kind.

Make a model to answer each question. Then draw a picture to record your work.

1. Show all the possible arrays for 10 cars.

2. Show all the possible arrays for 20 cars.

3. 2 out of every 6 cars are new cars.
   Out of 18 cars, how many cars are new?

Making a model can help you to solve a problem.

1 out of every 5 cars is a 2-door model. Out of 15 cars, how many are 2-door models?

You can use 15 toothpicks to model 15 cars.
Make groups of 5.

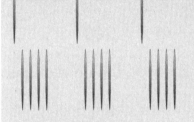

Then select 1 toothpick from each group.

So 3 out of 15 cars are 2-door models.

4. Amy had toy cars. She gave away her toy cars to Matt, Shani, and Vinh. They got 5 cars each. How many toy cars did Amy have?

7 Halving Strategies: Facts with 5 and 10

Goal Find patterns in multiplication and division facts with 5 and 10.

1. Show how 8 groups of 5 is the same as 4 groups of 10.

At–Home Help

You can use the **halve and double** strategy to find another fact using an easier fact.

$6 \times 5 = 30$ is the same as $3 \times 10 = 30$ because 3 is half of 6 and 10 is double 5.

2. Complete this Halve and Double table.

Multiply an even number by 5	Halve the even number and multiply by 10	Product
2×5	1×10	10
4		
6		
8		
10		
12		
14		
16		
18		

3. How could you use the table in Question 2 to find 7×5?

_____

_____

4. Complete.

a) $6 \times 5 =$ _____   d) $5 \times 80 =$ _____   g) $20 \div 10 =$ _____

b) $6 \times 50 =$ _____   e) $5 \times 800 =$ _____   h) $20 \div 5 =$ _____

c) $6 \times 500 =$ _____   f) $5 \times 8000 =$ _____

CHAPTER 6
8 Adding On: Facts with 3 and 6

Goal Use addition strategies to multiply and divide with 3 and 6.

1. Answer only the questions that are 3 or 6 facts.

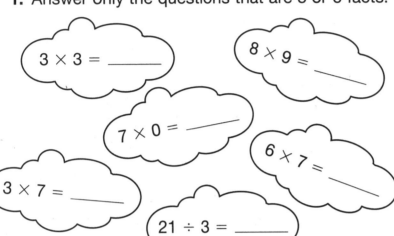

3 × 3 = _____

8 × 9 = _____

7 × 0 = _____

6 × 7 = _____

3 × 7 = _____

21 ÷ 3 = _____

At–Home Help

Facts you know can help you to find facts you don't know.

If you know 3 × 6 = 18, then 3 × 7 = 18 + 3
= 21

Counting on from a fact you know is a useful strategy to find a fact you can't remember.

6 × 5 = _____

5 × 7 = _____

3 × 8 = _____

4 × 9 = _____

42 ÷ 6 = _____

18 ÷ 3 = _____

2 × 8 = _____

12 ÷ 3 = _____

6 × 6 = _____

4 × 5 = _____

3 × 6 = _____

4 × 3 = _____

30 ÷ 6 = _____

Count the number of questions you answered.
If you counted 13, you answered all the questions with facts of 3 or 6.

2. a) What is the greatest answer you found? _____

b) Write a fact of 6 with an answer that is greater. _____

3. a) What is the least answer you found? _____

b) Write a division by 3 fact with an answer that is less. _____

9 Subtracting Strategy: Facts with 9

Goal Use counting patterns to multiply and divide with 9.

1. Complete the table.

Fact of 9	Fact of 10	Subtraction
1 × 9	1 × 10 = 10	10 − 1 = 9
2 × 9	2 × 10 = ____	20 − 2 = ____

At-Home Help

To multiply by 9, multiply the number by 10 and then subtract the number.

For example, 5 × 9 is the same as 5 × 10 − 5.

2. Use the subtraction strategy to find each product.

a) 4 × 9 = _____

b) 5 × 9 = _____

c) 9 × 3 = _____

d) 2 × 9 = _____

e) 8 × 9 = _____

f) 7 × 9 = _____

g) 5 × 90 = _____

h) 9 × 200 = _____

i) 9 × 6000 = _____

3. Gary has 9 baseball cards. Soo has 6 times as many cards. How many cards does Soo have?

4. Sara saved 3 box tops. James saved 9 times as many box tops. 25 box tops are needed for a prize. Has James saved enough box tops to get a prize?

Number Neighbours: Facts with 7 and 8

Goal Use facts you know to multiply and divide with 7 and 8.

1. Use the given fact to complete the other 2 facts.

At-Home Help

a) $8 \times 3 = 24$ $8 \times 2 =$ _____ $8 \times 4 =$ _____

b) $7 \times 6 = 42$ $7 \times 5 =$ _____ $7 \times 7 =$ _____

c) $8 \times 7 = 56$ $8 \times 6 =$ _____ $8 \times 8 =$ _____

d) $7 \times 4 = 28$ $7 \times 3 =$ _____ $7 \times 5 =$ _____

e) $8 \times 5 = 40$ $8 \times 4 =$ _____ $8 \times 6 =$ _____

f) $7 \times 8 = 56$ $7 \times 7 =$ _____ $7 \times 6 =$ _____

> Using a fact you know and then adding or subtracting can help you to find facts you don't know.
>
> Knowing 7×7 helps you to find the neighbour facts, 7×8 and 7×6.
>
> $7 \times 7 = 49$
> $7 \times 8 = \blacksquare$ $49 + 7 = 56$
> $7 \times 6 = \blacksquare$ $49 - 7 = 42$

2. Divide.

a) $28 \div 7 =$ _____   c) $35 \div 5 =$ _____

b) $48 \div 8 =$ _____   d) $72 \div 8 =$ _____

3. Multiply.

a) $7 \times 60 =$ _____   c) $8 \times 90 =$ _____

b) $8 \times 500 =$ _____   d) $7 \times 400 =$ _____

4. 36 stickers are shared evenly among 9 friends. How many stickers does each person receive?

5. Paulette walks 6 km each day. How many kilometres does she walk in 1 week?

Test Yourself

Circle the correct answer.

1. There are 6 paintbrushes in each of 7 pots.
   How many paintbrushes are there altogether?

   A. 13   **B.** 1   **C.** 42   **D.** 54

2. Ravi hands out 42 pieces of paper to 6 students.
   Each student gets the same amount of paper.
   How many pieces of paper does each student get?

   E. 8   **F.** 48   **G.** 36   **H.** 7

3. The paint tables are arranged like this.
   Which equation matches this array?

   A. $2 \times 5 = 10$ **B.** $5 + 2 = 10$ **C.** $10 \times 1 = 10$ **D.** $10 - 5 = 2$

4. There are 600 crayons in each bin.
   How many crayons are in 5 bins?

   E. 30   **F.** 300   **G.** 3000   **H.** 1100

5. Lance, Alice, and Rami painted 24 pictures.
   Each student painted the same number of pictures.
   How many pictures did each student paint?

   A. 8   **B.** 12   **C.** 27   **D.** 72

6. The art room has 8 tables. Each table seats 6 students.
   How many students can sit at the tables in the art room?

   E. 14   **F.** 48   **G.** 54   **H.** 2

7. 6 tables seat 6 students each.
   How many students will there be if 7 tables are filled?

   A. 36   **B.** 42   **C.** 30   **D.** 19

8. A group of 8 students made 72 decorations.
   Each student made the same number of decorations.
   How many decorations did each student make?

   E. 9   **F.** 8   **G.** 10   **H.** 80

1 Classifying Quadrilaterals

Goal Identify and sort quadrilaterals.

1. Which of these are parallelograms?

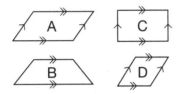

2. Which of these are trapezoids?

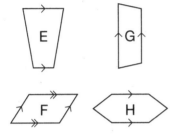

3. Draw a quadrilateral that is not a parallelogram or a trapezoid.

4. Draw a square. What other shape names can be used to describe a square?

At–Home Help

A quadrilateral is a closed shape with 4 straight sides.

A **trapezoid** has exactly 1 pair of parallel sides.

> or » indicates parallel sides.

A **parallelogram** has 2 pairs of parallel sides.

A rectangle, a square, and a rhombus are special parallelograms.

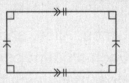

ı and ıı indicate equal sides.

2 Building Quadrilaterals

Goal Relate properties of quadrilaterals to their side lengths.

1. Use straws or toothpicks to make these shapes. Draw a picture of each shape. What type of quadrilateral is each shape?

   a) a quadrilateral with 4 equal sides and square corners

   b) a quadrilateral with 2 equal long sides and 2 equal short sides, but no square corners

   c) a quadrilateral with no equal sides, but 1 pair of parallel sides

   d) a quadrilateral with 3 equal sides, but no parallel sides

At-Home Help

Quadrilaterals can have 4, 3, 2, or no equal side lengths.

This shape has 3 equal side lengths.

Parallelograms have 2 pairs of equal side lengths.

3 Congruent Shapes

Goal Identify and construct congruent shapes.

1. Which shapes are congruent?

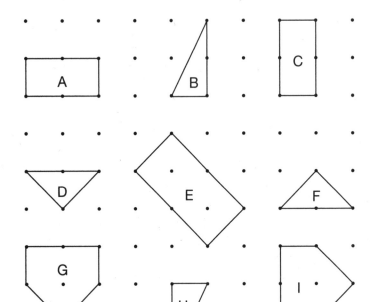

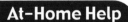

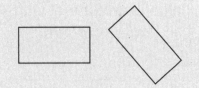

2. Construct a shape congruent to each shape on the grid, using the given line as one side.

a)

b)

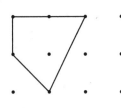

CHAPTER 7

4 Similar Shapes

Goal Identify and describe similar shapes.

1. Which shapes look similar to the first shape? Explain.

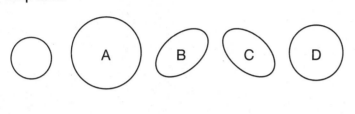

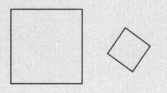
_____

_____

2. Which shapes look similar to the first shape? Explain.

_____

_____

3. Which shapes look similar to the first shape? Explain.

_____

_____

4. Janice says that congruent shapes are special similar shapes. Do you agree? Why or why not?

_____

_____

5 Measuring Angles

 Goal Measure angles using a protractor.

1. How many degrees is each angle?

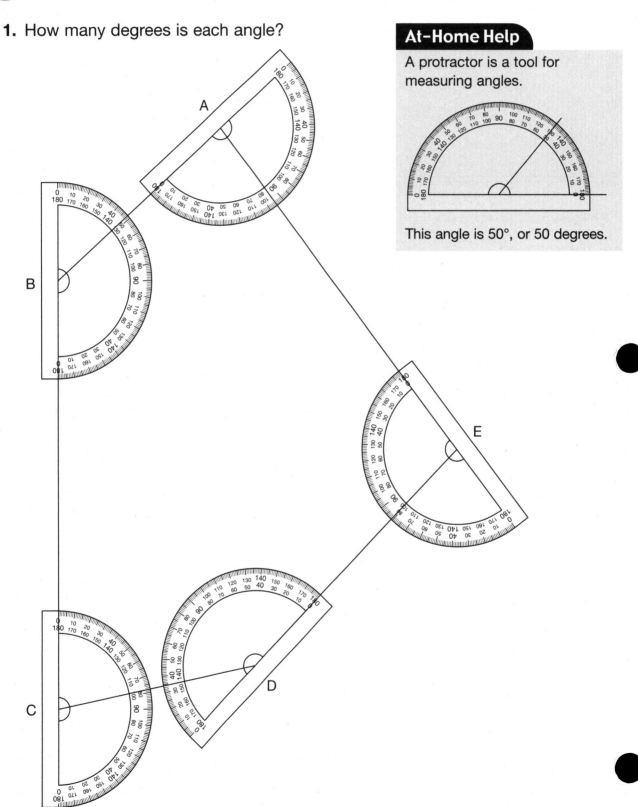

6 Solve Problems by Acting Them Out

Goal Act out a problem to solve it.

Trace this square and cut out the square you drew.

Cut out as many squares as you need to answer the questions below.

1. 6 square tables are arranged to make 1 long narrow table. 1 person sits on each outside edge of a square table. How many people can sit at the long table?
   Sketch your answer after you act it out.

2. How many squares does it take to make a bigger square?
   Find more than one answer. Sketch your answers after you act them out.

7 Lines of Symmetry

Goal Draw lines of symmetry.

1. Trace each shape and cut out the shape you drew.
Fold it to find a line of symmetry. Unfold it.
Repeat to find other lines of symmetry.
On this page, draw all the lines of symmetry
that you found for each shape.

At–Home Help

A **line of symmetry** is a line
that divides a shape in half so if
you fold the shape along the
line, the halves match.

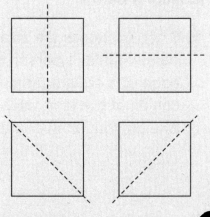

A square has 4 lines of
symmetry.

a)

b)

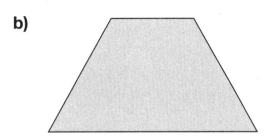

c)

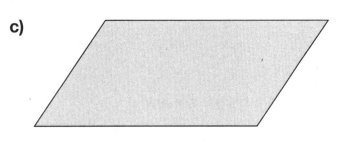

e)

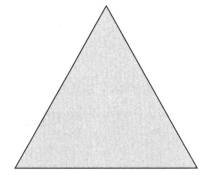

d)

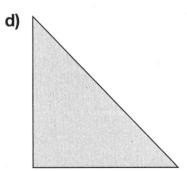

2. Which of the shapes in Question 1 has the most lines of symmetry?

How many? _____

Classifying 2-D Shapes

Goal Identify and sort 2-D shapes.

1.

At-Home Help

2-D shapes can be sorted, or classified, in many different ways. Some of the things you can consider are
- the number of sides
- whether any sides are equal in length
- whether the shapes are congruent
- whether there are any parallel sides
- whether there are square corners
- whether the shape has symmetry

a) Which shapes have parallel sides?

_____

b) Which shapes are similar? _____

c) Which shapes have symmetry? _____

2. Describe another way to sort the shapes in Question 1. Which shapes belong?

_____

_____

3. Draw 4 shapes of your own and show 2 ways to sort them.

Test Yourself

Circle the correct answer.

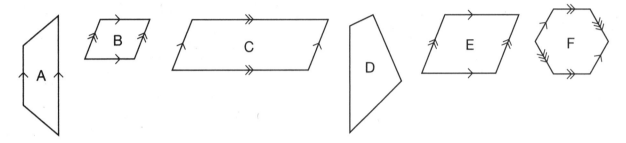

1. What type of shape is shape D?

   A. a quadrilateral   **B.** a trapezoid   **C.** a rhombus   **D.** a parallelogram

2. Which shape has more than 2 lines of symmetry?

   E. shape A   **F.** shape F   **G.** shape C   **H.** shape E

3. Which shape has no parallel sides?

   A. shape D   **B.** shape E   **C.** shape B   **D.** shape A

4. Which shape is similar to shape E?

   E. shape F   **F.** shape B   **G.** shape C   **H.** shape A

5. Which of these shapes is congruent to shape A?

   A.   **B.**    **C.** 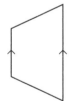   **D.**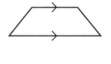

6. Which of these shape names is **not** another way of describing a square?

   E. a rectangle   **F.** a trapezoid   **G.** a parallelogram   **H.** a quadrilateral

7. What is the measure of the angle shown?

   A. 30°   **C.** 145°

   B. 35°   **D.** 150°

   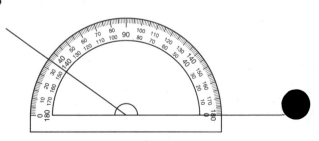

CHAPTER 8

1 Standard Area Units

Goal   **Explain why we use standard units to measure area.**

1. You want to estimate the area of your kitchen table. Choose the item that would be the best unit to measure this area. Explain your choice.

   A. a CD case   **B.** a piece of string   **C.** a plastic cup

   _____

   _____

> **At-Home Help**
>
> Measurement requires an understanding of what is being measured (length, area, capacity, and so on). Once that is understood an appropriate unit of measure can be chosen.
>
> Comparing measurements found using informal units, such as palms of hands, suggests the need for standard units.

2. Estimate the area of the surface of a table, desk, cutting board, or some other flat object. Measure the surface using a playing card, a paper napkin, an envelope, or another object that is square or rectangular. Record what surface you measured, what you used, and the area.

   _____

   _____

3. **a)** How many pillows is the area of the top surface of your bed?

   _____

   b) If you measured your bed using a different pillow, would your answer

   be the same? Why or why not? _____

   _____

4. Shani's family bought a new carpet for the living room. Before they bought the carpet, they measured the area of the floor. Give 2 other examples when an area measurement is needed.

   _____

   _____

Copyright © 2004 Nelson

Chapter 8: Area and Grids   **69**

2 Square Centimetres

Goal Estimate, measure, and compare area using square centimetres.

1. Measure the area of each shape to the nearest whole square centimetre.

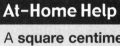

At-Home Help

A **square centimetre** is one standard unit for measuring area.

1 cm
1 cm

A square with sides of 1 cm has an area of one square centimetre.

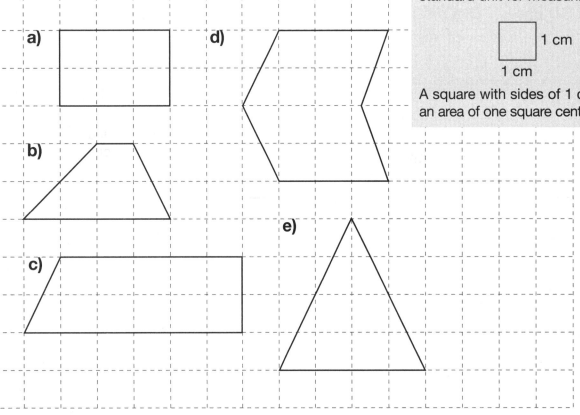

a)

b)

c)

d)

e)

2. List the shapes from Question 1 in order from greatest to least area,

using their letters. _____

3. Nisha thinks that both of these shapes have an area of 1 square centimetre. Is she correct? Explain why or why not.

_____

_____

_____

3 Square Metres

Goal Estimate area using an appropriate area unit.

1. Would you use a square metre or a square centimetre to measure each item?

   a) a school flag _____

   b) a playing card _____

   c) a helicopter landing pad _____

   d) a postcard _____

   e) a floor mat for gymnastics

   _____

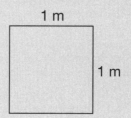
2. If you had 1 square metre of material, which of these items could you make?

   A. a Batman cape

   B. a tent large enough for a family of 4

   C. a curtain for the school stage

3. Which measurement would be the most reasonable estimate for the area of your bedroom floor?

   D. between 1 square metre and 4 square metres

   E. between 20 square metres and 30 square metres

   F. between 8 square metres and 15 square metres

4. A square metre is divided into 4 parts and used to make a new shape. What is the area of the new shape? Explain.

   _____

   _____

4 Relating Linear Dimensions and Area

Goal **Relate the area of a rectangle to its length and width.**

1. What is the area of each rectangle?

a)
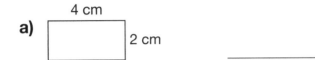
4 cm
2 cm

_____

At-Home Help

Area is measured by finding out how many square units are needed to cover the surface.

The area of a rectangle is related to its side lengths.

3 cm

5 cm

area = 3 cm × 5 cm
= 15 square centimetres

b)

4 cm
3 cm

_____

c)
4 cm
5 cm

_____

2. Complete the table.

Rectangle	Width	Length	Area
A	3 cm	2 cm	
B	7 cm		14 square centimetres
C	4 cm	6 cm	
D		7 cm	49 square centimetres

3. What is the length of the other side?

a)
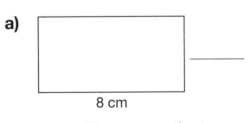
8 cm

area = 32 square centimetres

b)
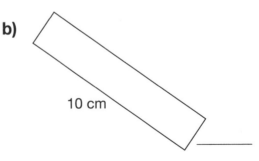
10 cm

area = 20 square centimetres

CHAPTER 8

5 Relating Shape, Area, and Perimeter

Goal Investigate how changes in shape affect area and perimeter.

1.

a) area:

_____

perimeter:

_____

b) area:

_____

perimeter:

_____

The shapes have the same _____.

2.

a) area:

_____

perimeter:

_____

b) area:

_____

perimeter:

_____

The shapes have the same _____.

At-Home Help

Shapes can have the same area but different perimeters.

5 cm

4 cm

area = 4 cm × 5 cm
     = 20 square centimetres

perimeter = 4 cm + 5 cm +
            4 cm + 5 cm
          = 18 cm

2 cm

10 cm

area = 10 cm × 2 cm
     = 20 square centimetres

perimeter = 10 cm + 2 cm +
            10 cm + 2 cm
          = 24 cm

Shapes can also have the same perimeter but different areas.

SAVONA ELEMENTARY SCHOOL
P.O. BOX 170
SAVONA, B.C
V0K 2J0

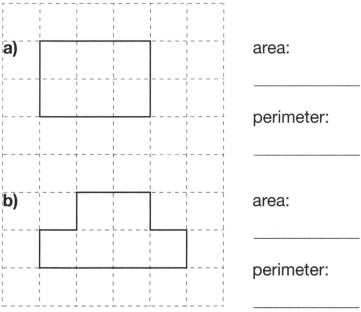

Solve Problems Using Organized Lists

 Goal Use an organized list to solve area problems.

1. How many different rectangles could you make with an area of 24 square tiles? What are they?

2. Sara chooses 3 numbers for the combination of her new bike lock. She uses 1, 4, and 7. She can use each number only once. What are the possible combinations?

At-Home Help

An **organized list** allows you to record information in a clear and organized way.

Vanessa has 35 cents. She has 2 of these 3 types of coins— quarters, dimes, and nickels. How many combinations of coins might she have?

25	10	5
1	1	0
1	0	2
0	3	1
0	2	3
0	1	5

There are 5 possible combinations.

3. Ben goes to the grocery store for his mom. He spends less than $5. He buys at least one of each of the following items.
   - apples at 50¢ each
   - bread at $1.60 a loaf
   - crackers at $1.25 a package
   Find all the combinations of what he might have bought.

Test Yourself Page 1

Circle the correct answer.

1. You want to estimate the area of the top surface of a desk. Which item would you use?

    A. a piece of string

    B. a measuring cup

    C. an envelope

    D. a balance scale

2. What is the area of this shape to the nearest whole square centimetre?

    E. 18 square centimetres

    F. 20 square centimetres

    G. 14 square centimetres

    H. 16 square centimetres

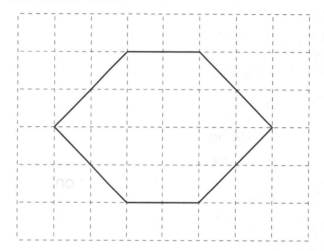

3. Which of the following would not be measured using square centimetres?

    A. a schoolyard

    B. a placemat

    C. a photograph

    D. a piece of note paper

4. Which measurement would be the most reasonable estimate for the area of your kitchen floor?

    E. between 1 square metre and 3 square metres

    F. between 10 square metres and 20 square metres

    G. between 30 square metres and 40 square metres

    H. between 40 square metres and 50 square metres

5. What is the area of this rectangle?

    A. 24 cm

    B. 24 square centimetres

    C. 10 cm

    D. 20 square centimetres

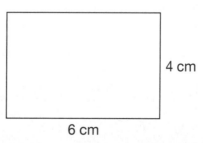

4 cm

6 cm

Circle the correct answer.

6. What is the length of the other side?

3 cm

area = 18 square centimetres

    E. 6 cm

    F. 15 cm

    G. 6 square centimetres

    H. 9 square centimetres

7. Which of these measurements is the same for the 2 rectangles?

    A. length

    B. width

    C. perimeter

    D. area

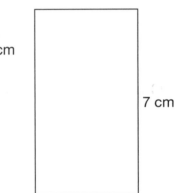

3 cm

8 cm

7 cm

4 cm

8. Which is true for the shape shown?

    E. area = 14 square centimetres
    perimeter = 8 centimetres

    F. area = 8 square centimetres
    perimeter = 14 centimetres

    G. area = 8 centimetres
    perimeter = 14 square centimetres

    H. area = 8 square centimetres
    perimeter = 8 centimetres

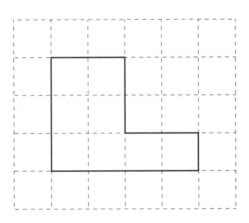

9. How many different rectangles can be made using exactly 28 square tiles placed side by side?

    A. 4   **B.** 5   **C.** 3   **D.** 8

10. Each of the digits 3, 5, and 6 is used only once to make a new number. How many different numbers can be made?

    E. 5   **F.** 3   **G.** 8   **H.** 6

1 Exploring Multiplication

Goal Solve multiplication problems using models.

1. Circle the letter of the problem that can be solved using multiplication.

   A. Rey read 22 pages on Monday, 29 pages on Tuesday, and 27 pages on Thursday. How many pages did he read altogether?

   B. Natalie read on Monday, Tuesday, and Thursday. She read 31 pages each day. How many pages did she read altogether?

   C. Paulette read 96 pages in total on Monday, Tuesday, and Thursday. How many pages did she read each day?

   D. Chantal read 37 pages on Monday. Vinh read 29 pages on Monday. How many more pages did Chantal read than Vinh?

> **At-Home Help**
>
> Multiplication involves groups of the same size.
>
> 4×28 is 4 groups of 28 objects. 28 groups of 4 has the same product.

   Explain how you know this problem can be solved using multiplication.

   _____

   _____

   _____

2. Solve the problem in Question 1 using multiplication.

3. Circle the letter that shows base ten blocks being used to model multiplication.

   A. ▯▯▯▯▫ ▯▯▯▯▫ ▯▯▯▯▫ ▯▯▯▯▫   **B.** ▯▯ ▦ ▯▯ ▫ ▯▯ ▦

   Explain how you know that the base ten blocks are being used to model multiplication.

   _____

   _____

2 Multiplying with Arrays

Goal Use easier numbers to simplify multiplication.

1. A kitchen floor has 8 rows and 17 columns of tiles. These arrays show 8×17 by showing $8 \times 10 + 8 \times 7$.

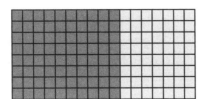

At-Home Help

Using easier numbers to multiply is useful when one factor is greater than 10.
$3 \times 18 = 3 \times 10 + 3 \times 8$
$3 \times 18 = 30 + 24$
$3 \times 18 = 54$

Or using other easier facts:
$3 \times 18 = 3 \times 9 + 3 \times 9$
$3 \times 18 = 27 + 27$
$3 \times 18 = 54$

$8 \times 17 =$ _____ + _____

$8 \times 17 =$ ____ + ____

$8 \times 17 =$ ____

2. Complete.

   a) $2 \times 56 = 2 \times 50 + 2 \times 6$

   $2 \times 56 =$ ____ + ____

   $2 \times 56 =$ ____

   b) $5 \times 14 = 5 \times 7 + 5 \times$ ____

   $5 \times 14 =$ ____ + ____

   $5 \times 14 =$ ____

   c) $4 \times 29 = 4 \times$ ____ $+ 4 \times$ ____

   $4 \times 29 =$ ____ + ____

   $4 \times 29 =$ ____

   d) $6 \times 22 =$ ____ $\times$ ____ $+$ ____ $\times$ ____

   $6 \times 22 =$ ____ + ____

   $6 \times 22 =$ ____

3. Find each product.

   a) 9×18

   b) 7×12

   c) 4×19

   d) 8×33

3 Multiplying in Expanded Form

Goal Multiply 1-digit numbers by 2-digit numbers using expanded form.

1. Complete.

a) 46 × 9

```
  4 tens +  6 ones
              × 9
 ─────────────────
 36 tens + 54 ones
 41 tens +  4 ones

 _____
```

c) 78 × 9

```
   70 + 8
      × 9
 ─────────
      630
    + 72

 ─────────
```

b) 89 × 5

```
  8 tens +  9 ones
              × 5
 ─────────────────
 40 tens + _____

 _____

 _____
```

d) 36 × 8

```
   30 + 6
      × 8
 ─────────
    _____

 +  _____

 ─────────
```

2. Stanley can display 37 models on 1 shelf. How many models can he display on 4 shelves?

3. Circle the letter that is a reasonable estimate for 96 × 5.

   A. more than 450   **B.** less than 450   **C.** less than 45   **D.** less than 30

   Explain how you know.

CHAPTER 9
4

Communicate About Solving Problems

Goal   **Explain your thinking when solving a problem.**

1. Name the steps that Chantal used to solve this problem.
   Chantal's baby brother is 17 weeks old. How many days old is he?

At-Home Help

Problem solving involves
• understanding the problem
• making a plan to solve the problem
• carrying out the plan
• looking back to check

Step 1 _____

My brother is 17 weeks old.
I know there are 7 days in 1 week.

Step 2 _____

I will multiply 17 and 7.

Step 3 _____

$$10 + 7$$
$$\underline{\times\ 7}$$
$$70$$
$$\underline{+\ 49}$$
$$119$$

My brother is 119 days old.

Step 4 _____

If my brother were 20 weeks old, he would be 140 days old. So 119 days is reasonable for 17 weeks old.

2. Show the steps as you solve each problem.

   a) At a party there are 36 tables. Each table will have 5 balloons. How many balloons will there be in all?

   b) It rained for 3 days. How many hours did it rain?

CHAPTER 9

5 Multiplying 3 Digits by 1 Digit

Goal **Multiply 3-digit numbers by 1-digit numbers using expanded form.**

1. Complete.

372 × 3 is about

_____

300 + 70 + 2
            × 3
_____

At-Home Help

Estimating helps you to check that your answers are reasonable.

298 × 5 is about 300 × 5, or 1500.

            200 + 90 + 8
                    × 5
            _____
                   1000
                    450
            +   40
            _____
                   1490

2. A bottle of vitamins contains 120 tablets. How many tablets are in 8 bottles? Circle the most reasonable estimate.

A. more than 800   **B.** less than 800   **C.** more than 1600   **D.** more than 80

Explain how you know.

3. Connor's family's cable bill is $126 every 2 months.

a) Estimate how much they pay in 1 year.

b) Calculate how much they pay in 1 year.

4. Jasmine often visits her grandmother on weekends. It is 247 km there and back.

a) Create a 1-digit by 3-digit multiplication problem about Jasmine's visits.

b) Estimate the answer.

c) Calculate the answer.

Copyright © 2004 Nelson

Chapter 9: Multiplying Greater Numbers   **81**

6 Multiplying with an Algorithm

Goal Multiply using a procedure.

1. Estimate each product.

a) 139 × 9

b) 358 × 8

c) 729 × 2

d) 298 × 5

e) 498 × 6

> **At–Home Help**
>
> One multiplication **algorithm**, or **procedure** to multiply, is this:
>
> $$\begin{array}{r} {\scriptstyle 3\,2} \\ 174 \\ \underline{\times\ 5} \\ \mathbf{870} \end{array}$$
>
> Because
> 4 ones × 5 = 20,
> or 2 tens **0 ones**.
> 7 tens × 5 + 2 tens more =
> 350 + 20 = 370, or
> 3 hundreds **7 tens**.
> 1 hundred × 5 + 3 hundreds
> more = 500 + 300 = 800,
> or **8 hundreds**.

2. You should have 3 estimates that are 1500 or less.
Calculate their products.

3. Estimate and then calculate.

a) 396
   × 7

b) 629
   × 5

CHAPTER 9

7

Choosing a Method to Multiply

 Goal **Choose and justify a multiplication method.**

Use these facts in the questions below.

- The average Canadian consumes 25 kg of fresh fruit in juices in 1 year.
- The average Canadian child watches 884 hours of TV in 1 year.
- A small roast beef submarine sandwich has 954 kilojoules of energy.

At-Home Help

Look at the question to decide if an estimate will do.
Look at the numbers in a problem to decide if you can solve it mentally or if you need to use pencil and paper.

1. You want to find out how many kilograms of fresh fruit in juices a family of 6 consumes in 1 year. Would you use pencil and paper or mental math? Explain your choice. Solve the problem.

2. You want to find out about how many hours of TV a child would watch in 9 years. Would you estimate or do an exact calculation? Explain your choice. Solve the problem.

3. You want to find out how many kilojoules of energy a person would get from eating 1 small roast beef submarine sandwich each day for a week. Would you use pencil and paper or mental math? Why? Solve the problem.

Test Yourself

Circle the correct answer.

1. What are these base ten blocks modelling?

   A. 140 ÷ 5   **B.** 5 × 29   **C.** 29 × 4   **D.** 30 + 30 + 30 + 30 + 30

2. Which multiplication equation is modelled by this array?

   E. 4 × 22 = 4 × 20 + 4 × 2   **G.** 4 × 20 = 4 × 10 + 4 × 10

   F. 23 × 4 = 20 × 4 + 3 × 4   **H.** 4 × 20 = 2 × 20 + 2 × 20

3. The array in Question 2 could be broken into other arrays.
   Which of these is possible?

   A. 4 × 9 + 4 × 14   **C.** 2 × 23 + 2 × 23

   B. 4 × 11 + 4 × 11   **D.** 25 × 4 + 3 × 4

4. Miki used expanded form. What problem was she solving?

   E. How many eggs are in 129 dozen?

   F. How many weeks are in 129 days?

   G. How many hours are in 7 days?

   H. How many days are in 129 weeks?

   ```
   100 + 20 + 9
            × 7
   _____
          700
          140
   +       63
   _____
          903
   ```

5. Which estimate is the most reasonable for the product
   of 389 × 4?

   A. 1200   **B.** 1600   **C.** 2000   **D.** 700

6. What is the product of 638 × 6?

   E. 3828   **F.** 3688   **G.** 3728   **H.** 3888

7. The average Canadian eats 183 kg of vegetables in 1 year.
   How much does a family of 4 eat in 2 years?

   A. 366 kg   **B.** 732 kg   **C.** 1464 kg   **D.** 1098 kg

1 Exploring Division

Goal Solve division problems using models.

You will need 40 bread tags, toothpicks, coins, buttons, or something else to use as counters.

At-Home Help

The number you divide by in a division equation is the divisor.

$8 \div 4 = 2$

divisor

1. Use counters. Show how 40 band members would group themselves as they march each way. Then sketch a diagram.

   a) 2 equal columns   **b)** 4 equal columns   **c)** 5 equal columns

2. Use counters. Can 40 band members group themselves in equal columns if they march each way? Why or why not?

   a) 6 columns _____

   b) 7 columns _____

   c) 8 columns _____

3. Use counters. There are between 25 and 35 students working in groups planting trees. Which numbers of students could there be in each case?

   a) All students are working in groups of 5. _____

   b) All students are working in groups of 4. _____

   c) All students are working in groups of 3. _____

4. What number in each part of Question 3 is the divisor?

   a) _____   **b)** _____   **c)** _____

Using Repeated Subtraction to Divide

Goal Use repeated subtraction to divide.

1. 72 muffins are to be put in packages of 5 muffins each. To find how many packages are needed, divide.

   5)72   ◄——— Start with 72 muffins
   −50 10 ◄— At least 10 packages are needed.
   22   ◄——— Now 22 muffins are left.
   −20   4 ◄— 4 more packages are needed
   2   ◄——— Now 2 muffins are left.

   10 + 4 = 14 packages are needed.
   But 2 muffins are left over.

   At-Home Help

   When dividing larger numbers, you can use **repeated subtraction**.

   If you need to find 102 ÷ 8, you know that the answer is at least 10 because 80 ÷ 8 = 10. Then you can subtract to see how many more are needed. (See Question 1 for an example.)

   a) How many muffins were there at the beginning? _____

   b) After they were packaged, how many muffins were left over? _____

   c) What is the number in part b) called? _____

   d) Which number is the divisor? _____

   e) Why was it known that at least 10 bags were needed? _____

   _____

   f) Why was it known that 4 more bags would be needed? _____

   _____

2. 72 muffins were put in packages of 6. How many packages are needed? How many muffins are left over?

3. Use repeated subtraction to divide. Show your steps.

   a) 4)49   b) 7)85   c) 3)39   d) 6)98

3 Interpreting Remainders

Goal Decide how to treat the remainder in a division problem.

1. 75 students travel by minivan to an amusement park. Each minivan can take 6 students. How many minivans are needed?

At-Home Help

The meaning of the remainder depends on what the problem asks.
4 different problems could be solved by 75 ÷ 6 = 12 R3.
The answers could be 12, 13, $12\frac{1}{2}$, and 3. (See an example of each in Questions 1 to 3.)

2. 75 slices of pizza were eaten. Each pizza was cut into 6 slices. How many pizzas were eaten?

3. 75¢ is to be shared equally among 6 students.

   a) How much will each student get?

   b) How much money will be left over?

4. Tickets costing $3 each were bought with $125.

   a) How many tickets were bought?

   b) How much was the change?

5. One car of an amusement park ride holds 4 people. 62 people take the ride. How many cars are needed?

6. 50 pictures are put in an album. Each page holds 4 pictures.

   a) Exactly how many pages are used?

   b) How many pages are full?

   c) How many pages are needed?

4 Dividing 2 Digits by 1 Digit

Goal Use base ten blocks and pencil and paper to divide a 2-digit number by a 1-digit number.

1. 5 people share 68 strawberries.

   a) Without dividing, tell if there will be any berries left over. How do you know?

   b) Estimate the number that each person will get.

   c) Sketch a picture to show the sharing.

   d) Record the division. Show all the steps.

   e) How many berries did each person get? How many were left over?

2. Divide. Show your work.

   a) $6\overline{)67}$ b) $5\overline{)56}$ c) $3\overline{)50}$ d) $8\overline{)93}$

At-Home Help

The number you divide into parts is the dividend.

$53 \div 4 = 13\ \text{R1}$
dividend

$\left.\begin{array}{r} 3 \\ 10 \end{array}\right\} 10 + 3 = 13$

$4\overline{)53}$
$\underline{-40}$
13
$\underline{-12}$
1

The remainder is 1.

5 Solve Problems By Guessing and Testing

Goal Use a guess-and-test strategy to solve problems.

1. Jalissa has 66 chairs to arrange for the show. She makes 5 equal rows and has 1 chair left over. How many chairs are in each row?

2. Derek has between 40 and 50 clothespins to put equally in 2 bags.

   a) How many clothespins could there be if there are none left over?

   b) How many clothes pins could there be if there is 1 left over?

3. Chloe has 87 books to place on 7 shelves. How many more books does she need to have an equal number on each shelf?

4. Ryan used between 50 and 60 cards to make an array with 4 rows. He has 1 card left over. How many cards did he start with? Find more than one answer.

At-Home Help

Guessing and testing is a useful strategy for solving problems. For example, a number between 25 and 35 is divided by 7 and the remainder is 3. To find the number, think:

$35 \div 7 = 5$, but there is no remainder.

$7 \times 4 = 28$

To have a remainder of 3, use $28 + 3 = 31$.

So $31 \div 7 = 4 \ R3$.

The number is 31.

---

6 Estimating with 3-Digit Dividends

Goal Use multiplication and division facts to estimate quotients.

1. Choose the correct answer.
To estimate $290 \div 7$, this fact is useful.

    A. $30 \div 5 = 6$ **C.** $28 \div 7 = 4$

    B. $27 \div 9 = 3$ **D.** $25 \div 5 = 5$

2. Choose the correct answer.
If I know $36 \div 4 = 9$, then I know _____.

    E. 36 tens $\div 4 = 90$ **G.** $360 \div 40 = 90$

    F. 36 tens $\div 4 = 9$ **H.** $360 \div 4 = 900$

> ### At-Home Help
>
> Using basic facts and extending them helps you to estimate quotients.
>
> For example, you know
> $18 \div 3 = 6$, so
> $180 \div 3 = 18$ tens $\div 3$
> $= 6$ tens
> $= 60$
> This helps you to estimate that $185 \div 3$ is about 60.

3. Doug wants to read a 168-page book in 6 days.

    a) What fact will help him to estimate how many pages he needs to read each day?

    b) About how many pages should he read each day?

4. Emma has

    • 125 blue beads   • 200 red beads   • 160 yellow beads

    To make 1 bracelet, she needs

    • 4 blue beads   • 6 red beads   • 5 yellow beads

    Estimate how many bracelets she can make with each colour of bead.

    a) blue   **b)** red   **c)** yellow

5. Estimate each quotient. Explain your thinking.

    a) $6\overline{)617}$ **b)** $8\overline{)509}$

CHAPTER 10

7 Dividing in Parts

Goal Divide in steps using simpler numbers.

1. Barb, Cameron, and Rory have coin collections. Barb has the greatest number, 390 coins. She has 5 times as many coins as Cameron. She has 3 times as many as Rory.

At-Home Help

285 ÷ 3 can be found by renaming 285 as 270 + 15 because 270 ÷ 3 is 90 and 15 ÷ 3 is 5.
So 285 ÷ 3 is 90 + 5, or 95.

a) Why is renaming 390 as 350 + 40 useful in finding out how many coins Cameron has?

b) Calculate $5\overline{)350}$ + $5\overline{)40}$.

c) How many coins does Cameron have?

d) Why is renaming 390 as 350 + 40 not useful in finding out how many coins Rory has?

e) Why is renaming 390 as 300 + 90 useful?

f) Why is renaming 390 as 360 + 30 useful?

g) Find the number of coins Rory has, using the renaming in part e) or f).

2. Divide into parts and find the quotient.

a) $6\overline{)618}$ b) $8\overline{)500}$ c) $5\overline{)710}$

8 Dividing 3 Digits by 1 Digit

Goal   Use base ten blocks and pencil and paper to divide a 3-digit number by a 1-digit number.

1. A class drinks 165 cartons of milk starting on Monday and ending on Friday. They drink the same number of cartons each day. How many cartons do the students drink each day?

At–Home Help

267 ÷ 7 = 38 R1

```
      38
  7)267
   -210
     57
   - 56
      1
```

2. 780 tickets were sold for 4 performances of a play.
   The same number of tickets were sold for each performance.
   How many tickets were sold for each performance?

3. Carolyn's class baked 276 cupcakes for a bake sale. They want to package all the cupcakes. Should they put them in packages of 6 or 8? Show your work.

4. Divide.

   a) 184 ÷ 4   c) 511 ÷ 7

   b) 336 ÷ 6   d) 616 ÷ 8

Test Yourself

Circle the correct answer.

1. Which division equation matches the diagram?

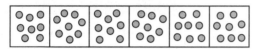

   A. 8 ÷ 6 = 48   **B.** 48 ÷ 8 = 8   **C.** 48 ÷ 8 = 6   **D.** 48 ÷ 12 = 4

2. 4 students are sharing 56 minutes of computer time equally. How many minutes does each student get?

   E. 14   **F.** 16   **G.** 18   **H.** 20

3. 57 students will receive certificates of achievement in mathematics. The certificates come in packages of 5. How many packages need to be bought?

   A. 8   **B.** 9   **C.** 10   **D.** 12

4. What is the remainder when 89 is divided by 8?

   E. 9   **F.** 1   **G.** 5   **H.** 11

5. 7 classes are sharing the planting of 500 spring bulbs equally. What is a reasonable estimate of the number of bulbs each class will plant?

   A. 30   **B.** 70   **C.** 90   **D.** 100

6. 132 students will be divided into teams of 4 for the science fair. How many teams will there be?

   E. 15   **F.** 27   **G.** 33   **H.** 44

7. 264 students are sitting in 8 equal rows for the assembly. How many students are in each row?

   A. 22   **B.** 33   **C.** 44   **D.** 55

8. Chloe is reading a 326-page book. She has read the same number of pages each day for 7 days. How many pages does she have left?

   E. 4   **F.** 6   **G.** 8   **H.** 10

1 Sketching Faces

Goal Describe relationships between 3-D shapes and their 2-D faces.

1. Try to find an item with each shape around your home. Name each item.

   a) rectangle-based prism _____

   b) triangle-based prism _____

   c) square-based pyramid _____

2. a) Record the shapes that you found in Question 1 in the chart below.
   b) Choose 1 item. Count the edges of your shape. Record the number in the chart.
   c) Trace each face of your shape. Find the total number of sides of all its faces.
   d) If you found any other shapes, repeat parts b) and c) for each one.

A **prism** has 2 bases.

A **pyramid** has 1 base.

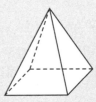

Prisms and pyramids are named by the shape of their bases. This box is a **rectangle-based prism**.

3-D shape	Total number of edges of 3-D shape	Total number of sides of 2-D faces
triangle-based pyramid	6	12

3. How is the total number of sides of the faces related to the number of edges? _____

_____

94 Chapter 11: 3-D Geometry and 3-D Measurement Copyright © 2004 Nelson

Building 3-D Shapes with Congruent Faces

Goal Build 3-D shapes and describe relationships between faces and vertices.

You will need scissors and tape.

At–Home Help

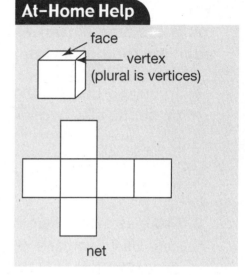
face
vertex
(plural is vertices)

net

1. Circle the letter of the shape that could be a net for a 3-D shape.

   A.

   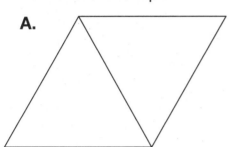

   B.

   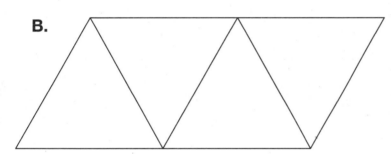

2. Trace the shape that could be a net onto a sheet of paper. Cut out and fold the net. Tape it together. Circle the letter of the 3-D shape you made.

   C. sphere   **E.** triangle-based pyramid

   D. triangle-based prism   **F.** cube

3. **a)** How many faces does the shape have? _____

   b) How many vertices does the shape have? _____

   c) How many faces meet at each vertex? _____

3 Making Skeleton Models

Goal Build 3-D skeletons and describe relationships between edges and vertices.

You will need toothpicks and modelling clay, miniature marshmallows, or something else to stick the toothpicks into.

At-Home Help

A **skeleton** of a 3-D shape has only edges and vertices.

1. To build 3-D skeletons, you can use modelling clay or miniature marshmallows to

   represent _____ and toothpicks to

   represent _____ .

2. Make as many skeletons of 3-D shapes as you can. Use 4 vertices, 5 vertices, and 6 vertices. Count the edges in each shape. Record each shape in the chart.

Shape number	Number of vertices	Number of edges
1	4	
2		
3		
4		
5		

3. For which number of vertices could you make more than 1 shape?

   _____

4. Did any of your shapes have more vertices than edges? _____

5. Did any of your shapes have the same number of vertices as edges?

   _____

4 Drawing 3-D Shapes

Goal **Draw prisms and pyramids.**

1. Find a rectangular prism such as a box.
   a) Draw the box so that you can see more than 1 face. Mark something on the visible faces to identify them.

At-Home Help

A drawing of a 3-D shape shows more than 1 face but it can't show all the faces.

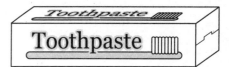

   b) Turn the box a different way. Draw it this way.

2. Draw a triangular prism on this triangular dot paper.

```
 .   .   .   .   .   .   .   .   .   .   .   .   .   .
   .   .   .   .   .   .   .   .   .   .   .   .   .
   .   .   .   .   .   .   .   .   .   .   .   .   .
   .   .   .   .   .   .   .   .   .   .   .   .   .
   .   .   .   .   .   .   .   .   .   .   .   .   .
   .   .   .   .   .   .   .   .   .   .   .   .
```

5 Communicate an Understanding of Geometric Concepts

Goal Use math language to show what you know about a 3-D shape.

1. Consider the shape of the building you live in. No matter where you live, the building has at least one 3-D shape. Describe the building.

_____

_____

_____

_____

_____

_____

_____

2. Use the Communication Checklist.
   a) What do you like about your description?

   _____

   _____

   _____

   _____

   _____

   b) How could you improve your description?

   _____

   _____

   _____

   _____

6 Measuring Mass

Goal **Estimate, measure, and record the mass of objects.**

1. Shani bought these items at the grocery store.

   500 g of potato salad   1 kg of apples
   400 g of sliced turkey   750 g of yogurt

   a) Order the masses from least to greatest.

   _____

   b) What combinations of items have a mass

   greater than 2 kg? _____

   _____

   _____

   c) Find the total mass of the items. Record the total mass in grams
   and kilograms.

   grams _____   kilograms _____

> **At–Home Help**
>
> **Mass** is the measure of matter in an object. The amount of matter determines how heavy the object is.
>
> Mass is measured in grams (g) and kilograms (kg).
> 1000 g = 1 kg

2. One litre (1 L) of water has a mass of 1 kg.

   a) Locate a light container that holds 1 L. You can use, for example,
   a 1 L juice or milk carton. If the container is full, it's close enough to
   1 kg for estimating. You can also use a 2 L container that is half full.

   b) List 6 items that are lighter than 1 kg. _____

   _____

   c) List 6 items that are heavier than 1 kg. _____

   _____

   d) Estimate the mass of 1 or 2 of the items in part b). Take the items
   to school tomorrow to measure their masses.

   _____

   _____

7 Measuring Capacity

Goal **Estimate, measure, and record the capacity of containers.**

You will need several empty containers that do not have capacity marked in litres or millilitres. Use items like glasses, cups, mugs, bowls, bottles, cartons, cans, and vases. You will also need a measuring cup marked in millilitres (250 mL or 500 mL).

At-Home Help

Capacity is the amount a container will hold when it is full. Capacity is measured in millilitres (mL) and litres (L). 1000 mL = 1 L

1. **a)** Examine your containers. Do not measure. Sort them into 2 groups.

   Group 1: containers that will hold less than my measuring cup

   Group 2: containers that will hold more than my measuring cup

   _____   _____

   _____   _____

   _____   _____

   _____   _____

   b) Which container will hold the least? _____

   c) Which container will hold the most? _____

   d) Which container will hold 1 L? _____

2. Fill one of your containers with water. Pour the water into your measuring cup, 1 cupful at a time. Record the number of millilitres to the nearest 50 mL. When you have done this for all your containers, check your answers to Question 1.

Container	Capacity to nearest 50 mL

CHAPTER 11

8 Using Mass and Capacity

Goal Choose appropriate capacity and mass units.

1. Which unit, grams or kilograms, would be most appropriate for measuring the mass of each item?

   At-Home Help

   mass: 1000 g = 1 kg
   capacity: 1000 mL = 1 L

   a) an ant _____

   b) an elephant _____   **e)** a pencil _____

   c) a picnic table _____   **f)** a feather _____

   d) a person _____   **g)** a bag of apples _____

2. Which unit, millilitres or litres, would be most appropriate for measuring the capacity of each item?

   a) a car's fuel tank_____   **e)** a mug _____

   b) a soup spoon _____   **f)** a swimming pool _____

   c) a picnic cooler _____   **g)** a drinking straw _____

   d) a bathtub _____

3. Find an item at home with its mass labelled in grams or kilograms.

   Is it labelled in the units you would expect? Explain. _____

   _____

4. Find an item at home with its capacity labelled in millilitres or litres.

   Is it labelled in the units you would expect? Explain. _____

   _____

Copyright © 2004 Nelson

Chapter 11: 3-D Geometry and 3-D Measurement **101**

9 Modelling Volume

Goal Model 3-D shapes to measure volume.

1. What is the volume of each 3-D shape?

a) 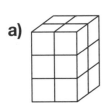 _____

b)  _____

c) 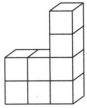 _____

At-Home Help

Volume is the measure of the amount of space taken up by a 3-D shape.

This shape has a volume of 7 cubes.

2. The volume of this 3-D shape is 5 toothpaste boxes.

Locate 2, 3, or 4 boxes that are the same size.
Create a 3-D shape using the boxes.

What is the volume of your 3-D shape? _____

Test Yourself

Circle the correct answer.

1. Which package shape can you find most often in your kitchen cupboard?

   A. a rectangle-based prism   **C.** a square-based pyramid

   B. a triangle-based prism   **D.** a triangle-based pyramid

2. What shape are the non-base faces of a prism?

   E. triangle   **F.** square   **G.** rectangle   **H.** cube

3. What shape are the non-base faces of a pyramid?

   A. triangle   **B.** square   **C.** rectangle   **D.** cube

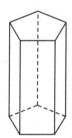

4. What is the name of this shape?

   E. square-based prism   **G.** pentagon-based prism

   F. triangle-based pyramid   **H.** pentagon-based pyramid

5. Which of these descriptions is true for the shape in Question 4?

   A. 5 faces, 10 edges, 10 vertices   **C.** 7 faces, 10 edges, 15 vertices

   B. 7 faces, 10 edges, 10 vertices   **D.** 7 faces, 15 edges, 10 vertices

6. What type of shape is this?

   E. triangle-based prism skeleton with more edges than vertices

   F. rectangle-based prism skeleton with 6 vertices

   G. rectangle-based prism skeleton with 9 edges

   H. triangle-based prism skeleton with 6 edges and 9 vertices

7. Estimate the amount of water in the bottle.

   A. 1 L   **B.** 500 mL   **C.** 750 mL   **D.** 250 mL

8. Which unit would you use to measure the capacity of a soup can?

   E. millilitres   **F.** grams   **G.** kilograms   **H.** litres

9. Which unit would you use to measure the mass of a soup can?

   A. millilitres   **B.** grams   **C.** kilograms   **D.** litres

1 Fractions of an Area

Goal Describe and compare fractions as part of an area using words, objects, pictures, and symbols.

1. Circle the letter of each cake top that shows fourths.

A.

B.

C.

D.

E.

2. a) Make this rectangular cake top $\frac{1}{2}$ red and $\frac{1}{4}$ blue.

   b) Write the fraction for the part that is not coloured. _____

3. Which fraction is greater? Tell how you know.

   a) $\frac{5}{6}$ or $\frac{1}{6}$ _____

   b) $\frac{3}{8}$ or $\frac{7}{8}$ _____

4. Join the dots in order from the least to the greatest.

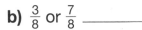
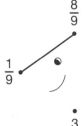

5. Is $\frac{1}{2}$ of cake top A the same as $\frac{1}{2}$ of cake top B? Explain.

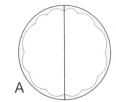

A   B

_____

_____

2 Mixed Numbers and Improper Fractions

Goal Model, write, and compare improper fractions and mixed numbers.

1. The trapezoid is the whole.

   a) Colour $3\frac{2}{3}$ trapezoids.

   b) How many triangles did you colour? _____

   c) Write the improper fraction that describes how much is coloured. _____

2. The rhombus is the whole.

   a) Colour $\frac{4}{2}$ rhombuses.   b) Colour $\frac{7}{2}$ rhombuses.

   c) Which is greater, $\frac{4}{2}$ or $\frac{7}{2}$? How do you know? _____

   _____

3. The trapezoid is the whole.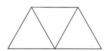

   a) Colour $4\frac{1}{3}$ trapezoids. Then write the improper fraction. _____

   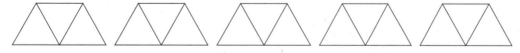

   b) Colour $\frac{5}{3}$ trapezoids. Then write the mixed number. _____

   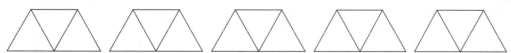

   c) Which is greater, $4\frac{1}{3}$ or $\frac{5}{3}$? How do you know? _____

   _____

3 Fractions of a Set

Goal Describe parts of sets using proper and improper fractions and mixed numbers.

Use toothpicks, bread tags, or other counters to help you if necessary.

At–Home Help

Mixed numbers and improper fractions can be used to describe parts of sets. For example, eggs come in cartons of 12.
14 eggs could be described as a mixed number, $1\frac{2}{12}$, or as an improper fraction, $\frac{14}{12}$.

1. Liza is writing thank-you cards. They come in packages of 8. She has used $1\frac{3}{8}$ of a package.

   a) How many cards has she used? _____

   b) What improper fraction describes $1\frac{3}{8}$

   of a package? _____

2. Mollie is putting pop cans in cartons. She puts 12 cans in each carton.

   a) Write the mixed number that describes how many cartons she can

   fill with 37 cans. _____

   b) Write this amount as an improper fraction. _____

3. Write the mixed number for each improper fraction.
   Then draw pictures of toothpicks to show the mixed number
   as sets and parts of sets.

   a) $\frac{15}{10}$ _____   b) $\frac{21}{8}$ _____   c) $\frac{14}{7}$ _____

4. Arrange these numbers in order from least to greatest.

   a) $\frac{6}{3}, \frac{1}{3}, \frac{4}{3}, \frac{8}{3}, \frac{10}{3}$ _____

   b) $1\frac{1}{5}, \frac{4}{5}, 2\frac{4}{5}, \frac{7}{5}, \frac{15}{5}$ _____

CHAPTER 12

4 Decimal Tenths

Goal Write decimal tenths using words and symbols.

1. Complete the chart.

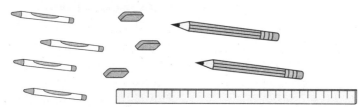

<table>
<tr><th>Item</th><th>Fraction of items</th><th>Decimal</th><th>Words</th></tr>
<tr><td>pencils</td><td>$\frac{2}{10}$</td><td>0.2</td><td>two tenths</td></tr>
<tr><td>erasers</td><td></td><td></td><td></td></tr>
<tr><td>crayons</td><td></td><td></td><td></td></tr>
<tr><td>rulers</td><td></td><td></td><td></td></tr>
<tr><td>glue sticks</td><td></td><td></td><td></td></tr>
</table>

At-Home Help

Decimals are a way to describe fractions. The fraction $\frac{2}{10}$ is written **0.2** and read **two tenths**. A decimal point separates the ones place from the fractional part. The 0 means there is no whole amount and the 2 is the numerator in the fraction $\frac{2}{10}$.

2. Write each decimal as a fraction.

   a) 0.2 _____ **b)** 1.0 _____ **c)** 0.9 _____

3. Write each fraction as a decimal. Then write it in words.

   a) $\frac{1}{10}$ _____ **b)** $\frac{0}{10}$ _____ **c)** $\frac{5}{10}$ _____

   _____ _____ _____

4. Draw and colour a design on the strip following the directions given.

   a) Put stars in less than $\frac{4}{10}$ of the boxes. Write the decimal amount of stars. _____

   b) Put triangles in more than $\frac{1}{2}$ of the boxes. Write the decimal amount of triangles. _____

   c) Colour almost all of the boxes. Write the decimal amount of coloured boxes. _____

   d) Write the decimals closest to

   0 _____ $\frac{1}{2}$ _____   1 _____

5 Decimal Tenths Greater Than 1

Goal Model, write, and compare decimal tenths greater than 1.

Use the metre sticks on the side of the page to help you.

1. Find 1.5 m on the metre sticks.

   a) What does the 1 in 1.5 m tell you?

   _____

   b) What does the 5 in 1.5 m tell you?

   _____

   c) Write 1.5 in words. _____

   _____

   d) How many decimetres is 1.5 m? _____

   e) Write 1.5 m as a mixed number. _____

2. Write a decimal for each mixed number. Then find each length in metres on the metre stick. The first one is done for you.

   a) $2\frac{1}{10}$ _____   **d)** $2\frac{4}{10}$ _____

   b) $1\frac{6}{10}$ _____   **e)** $1\frac{2}{10}$ _____

   c) $2\frac{8}{10}$ _____   **f)** $1\frac{9}{10}$ _____

3. Write each measurement in metres using decimals.

   a) one metre four decimetres _____

   b) twenty-five decimetres _____

   c) two metres eight decimetres _____

4. Arrange these measurements from longest to shortest.
   1.0 m, 2.2 m, 3.0 m, 1.8 m, 2.3 m, 1.2 m

At-Home Help

The drawing below shows 3 metre sticks end-to-end. The decimal marked A is 2.1 m. This represents 2 whole metres and 1 tenth of a metre, or 2 whole metres and 1 decimetre (1 dm).

6 Adding Decimal Tenths

Goal **Add decimals in tenths.**

Use the number line on the side of the page to help you with the questions.

At-Home Help

To add decimals, use the number line. For example, to add 2.9 and 2.1:
- Start at 2.9. (It's marked A.)
- Jump 2.0 from 2.9 to 4.9. (It's marked B.)
  That's 2 wholes added.
- Jump 0.1 more from 4.9 to 5.0. (It's marked C.)
  That's 1 tenth added.

$2.9 + 2.1 = 5.0$

1. **a)** Find 2.5 on the number line. Add 1.0 to it.

   What is the answer? _____

   b) Find 3.6 on the number line. Add 2.2 to it.

   What is the answer? _____

   c) Find 3.9 on the number line. Add 1.8 to it.

   What is the answer? _____

2. Add the lengths.

   a) 2.3 m and 1.8 m

   _____

   b) 3.0 km and 1.4 km

   _____

   c) 4.3 m and 1.2 m

   _____

   d) 2.8 m and 0.6 m _____

   e) 5.3 cm and 0.8 cm

   _____

   f) 4.0 m and 1.9 m

   _____

   g) 2.7 dm and 2.7 dm

   _____

3. Larry walked 3.5 km and then ran 2.2 km. How far did he go?

4. Find 4 different pairs of decimal tenths that add to 4.0.

5. Find 4 different pairs of decimal tenths that add to 6.1.

CHAPTER 12

7 Subtracting Decimal Tenths

Goal Subtract decimals in tenths.

Use the number line on the side of the page to help you.

To answer the riddle "What happens to a duck when it flies upside down?":
- find each difference
- use the code below to match each difference with a letter

1. $4.0 - 0.9 =$ _____

2. $3.0 - 1.9 =$ _____

3. $5.0 - 2.0 =$ _____

4. $4.0 - 1.3 =$ _____

5. $2.0 - 0.5 =$ _____

6. $3.8 - 1.2 =$ _____

7. $4.3 - 3.6 =$ _____

8. $5.2 - 4.8 =$ _____

9. $4.9 - 2.2 =$ _____

10. $4.6 - 2.3 =$ _____

At-Home Help

Count on to subtract decimal tenths. To subtract $1.3 - 0.6$:
- Find 0.6 on the number line. (It's marked A.)
- Count to 1.0. (It's marked B.). That's 4 tenths.
- Count from 1.0 to 1.3. (It's marked C.) That's another 3 tenths.

4 tenths and 3 tenths is 7 tenths, or 0.7.
So $1.3 - 0.6 = 0.7$.

Code

1.5	2.6	3.1	2.7	3.0	1.1	0.7	0.4	2.3
A	C	I	U	Q	T	K	S	P

____ ____   ____ ____ ____ ____ ____ ____   ____ ____

1. **2.**   **3.** **4.** **5.** **6.** **7.** **8.**   **9.** **10.**

11. The difference between the lengths of the front foot and the back foot of a skunk is 1.5 cm. Circle the letter of the lengths the feet could be.

    A. 4.0 cm and 1.5 cm   **C.** 3.0 cm and 1.5 cm

    B. 3.5 cm and 0.5 cm   **D.** 1.0 cm and 0.5 cm

12. A black bear's front foot is 14.0 cm long. A grizzly bear's front foot is 11.5 cm long. What is the difference between the lengths of their front feet? Use a ruler to help you.

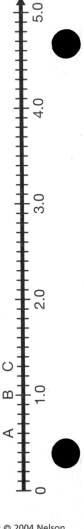

8 Communicate About Decimal Operations

Goal Use a model to explain how to add and subtract decimals.

1. These base ten blocks show the difference between 3.2 and 1.8.

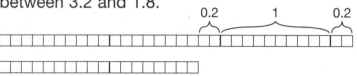

0.2 + 1 + 0.2 = 1.4

Check the answer by adding 1.8 and 1.4.

2. These base ten blocks show the difference between 4.1 and 2.6.

   a) Write an explanation using a diagram to show how the difference is found. Use the Communication Checklist to check your explanation.

   b) What is the difference? _____

   c) What could you add to check? _____

   d) Check.

3. These base ten blocks show the sum of 1.6 and 2.7.

   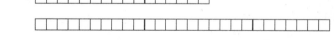

   a) How many rods are there altogether? _____

   b) How many cubes are there altogether? _____

   c) Express the number of cubes in part b) as rods and cubes. _____

   d) What is the sum of 1.6 and 2.7? _____

Decimal Hundredths Less Than or Equal to 1

Goal Write hundredths as decimals using words and symbols.

1. Write each fraction as a decimal and in words.

   a) $\frac{23}{100}$ _____

   b) $\frac{4}{100}$ _____

   c) $\frac{99}{100}$ _____

At-Home Help

32 hundredths of this grid is shaded. This is 0.32 or $\frac{32}{100}$.
68 hundredths of this grid is not shaded. This is 0.68 or $\frac{68}{100}$.

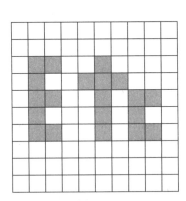

2. Order the decimals in Question 1 from least to greatest. _____

3. Write each decimal as a fraction.

   a) 0.52 _____   **b)** 0.07 _____   **c)** 0.89 _____

4. Write the decimal from Question 3 that is closest to each number.

   a) 1 _____   **b)** 0 _____   **c)** $\frac{1}{2}$ _____

5. Describe using fractions, decimals, and words.

   a) E _____

   _____

   b) t _____

   _____

   c) c _____

   _____

   d) Etc _____

   e) part not shaded _____

10 Add and Subtract Hundredths

Goal Add and subtract decimal hundredths using grids and calculators.

1. This 100 grid shows 0.42 + 0.29.

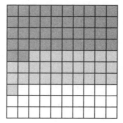

a) What is the sum?

_____

b) Explain how you know. _____

_____

At–Home Help

A 100 grid can be used to add decimal hundredths. Shade the number of squares equal to each decimal number. Then count all the shaded squares. (See Question 1.)

A 100 grid can be used to subtract decimal hundredths. One way is to shade the number of squares equal to the greater decimal number. Stroke out the number of shaded squares that is equal to the lesser number. Then count the shaded squares that didn't get stroked out. (See Question 2.)

2. This 100 grid shows 0.42 − 0.29.

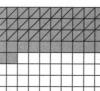

a) What is the difference?

_____

b) Explain how you know. _____

_____

3. Add or subtract using the 100 grids provided. If you have a calculator, check your answers.

a) 0.18 + 0.44

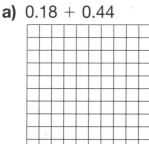

c) 0.53 + 0. 21

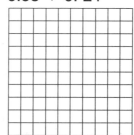

e) 0.75 − 0.10

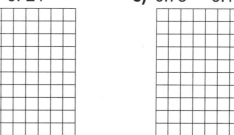

b) 0.52 − 0.20

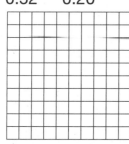

d) 0.66 − 0.22

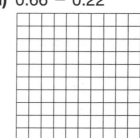

f) 0.38 + 0.38

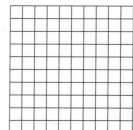

11 Relating Fractions and Decimals

Goal Explore, model, and calculate how fractions and decimals are related.

1. a) Shade $\frac{1}{2}$.

   $\frac{1}{2}$ as a decimal hundredth

   = _____

   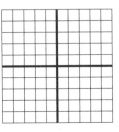

   b) Shade $\frac{3}{4}$.

   $\frac{3}{4}$ as a decimal hundredth

   = _____

   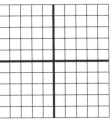

   c) Shade $\frac{1}{5}$.

   $\frac{1}{5}$ as a decimal hundredth

   = _____

   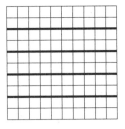

   d) Shade $\frac{2}{5}$.

   $\frac{2}{5}$ as a decimal hundredth

   = _____

   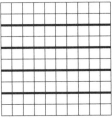

   e) Shade $\frac{3}{5}$.

   $\frac{3}{5}$ as a decimal hundredth

   = _____

   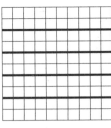

   f) Shade $\frac{4}{5}$.

   $\frac{4}{5}$ as a decimal hundredth

   = _____

   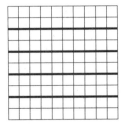

At-Home Help

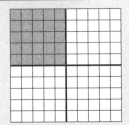

The grid is $\frac{1}{4}$ shaded. This is 25 hundredths of the grid, or 0.25.

$\frac{1}{4}$ = 0.25

You can check by dividing the numerator 1 by the denominator 4 using a calculator.

If you have a calculator, check that each decimal hundredth is correct. Divide the numerator of each fraction by its denominator.

Test Yourself Page 1

Circle the correct answer.

1. Which statement does **not** describe this rectangle?

    A. $\frac{3}{4}$ of the rectangle is shaded.

    B. $\frac{1}{3}$ of the rectangle is not shaded.

    C. Each section is $\frac{1}{4}$ of the whole area even though the sections are not the same shape.

    D. $\frac{1}{4}$ of the rectangle is not shaded.

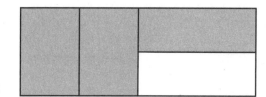

2. Which is a mixed number that describes the amount of hexagons that are shaded?

    E. $\frac{7}{2}$ **G.** $3\frac{1}{2}$

    F. $3\frac{1}{8}$ **H.** $\frac{3}{2}$

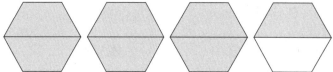

3. Juice boxes come in packages of 3. John has 14 juice boxes. Which fraction shows how many packages he has?

    A. $\frac{13}{3}$ packages   **B.** $4\frac{2}{3}$ packages   **C.** $\frac{3}{3}$ packages   **D.** $\frac{4}{3}$ packages

4. Which of the following correctly describes this set of pattern blocks?

    E. 0.01 of the set are trapezoids.

    F. The triangles and hexagons are more than 0.5 of the set.

    G. 4.0 of the set are rhombuses.

    H. The rhombuses and trapezoids are more than 0.4 of the set.

5. Which of the following shows the decimal amount shaded?

    A. 12.0   **C.** 1.2

    B. 1.12   **D.** 0.12

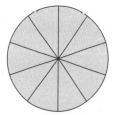
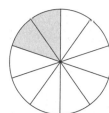

Circle the correct answer.

6. What is the sum of 3.8 and 4.2?

    E. 8.0   **F.** 7.10   **G.** 7.0   **H.** 0.4

7. What is the difference between 5.2 and 3.7?

    A. 8.9   **B.** 1.5   **C.** 1.3   **D.** 1.2

8. What operation is shown by these base ten blocks?

    E. $2.2 - 0.3 = 2.5$ **G.** $2.2 - 0.3 = 1.9$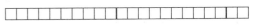

    F. $2.2 + 0.3 = 2.5$ **H.** $2.2 + 0.3 = 1.9$  $0.7 + 1 + 0.2$

9. What is $\frac{3}{100}$ as a decimal?

    A. 0.3   **B.** 3.0   **C.** 0.03   **D.** 0.30

10. What operation is shown on this grid?

    E. $0.43 + 0.19 = 0.62$

    F. $0.43 - 0.19 = 0.24$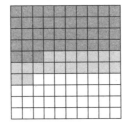

    G. $0.43 + 0.19 = 0.24$

    H. $0.43 - 0.19 = 0.62$

11. What operation is shown on this grid?

    A. $0.27 + 0.15 = 0.42$

    B. $0.27 - 0.15 = 0.42$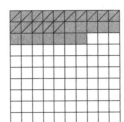

    C. $0.27 + 0.15 = 0.12$

    D. $0.27 - 0.15 = 0.12$

12. Which decimal represents $\frac{1}{4}$ on a calculator or on a 100 grid?

    E. 0.4   **F.** 0.25   **G.** 1.4   **H.** 0.40

1 Probability Lines

Goal Use a probability line to compare the probability of events.

1. Use words to describe the probability of each event.

   A I will eat soup for lunch tomorrow.

   _____

   B I will stay up until midnight tonight.

   _____

   C I will see a dinosaur walk past the school tomorrow.

   _____

   D I will watch TV tonight.

   _____

   E I will brush my teeth before going to bed tonight.

   _____

   F I will see a dog in the next week.

   _____

> ### At-Home Help
>
> We use probability words in our everyday language.
>
> When we are sure something will happen, we say **certain** or **always**.
>
> When we are sure something will not happen, we say **never** or **impossible**.
>
> Many events fall in between never and always. For these events, we use words such as **very unlikely**, **unlikely**, **possible**, **likely**, and **very likely**.

2. Place the letter for each event on the probability line.

   ←——————————————————————————————→
   impossible   certain

3. Create 3 of your own events and place their letters on the probability line.

   G _____

   H _____

   I _____

CHAPTER 13
2 Experimenting with Spinners

Goal Make predictions and experiment with spinners with equal sections.

1. Gen is at a fun fair. She will win a prize if she spins a 1 on Spinners A and B. Gen spun one of the spinners 20 times. Her results were: 1, 2, 1, 2, 3, 4, 3, 4, 2, 2, 1, 4, 3, 1, 4, 4, 3, 2, 3, 4.

> **At–Home Help**
>
> When a spinner has sections that are equal in size, the probability of landing on each section is equal. Each section has an equal chance of being spun.

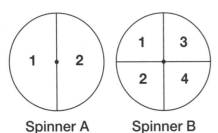

Spinner A   Spinner B

a) Which spinner did Gen spin? _____

b) Did Gen pick the right spinner to win as many prizes as she could in 20 spins? Explain. _____

_____

2. Predict the number of times Spinner X will spin an

   even number in 20 spins. _____

3. Use probability words to describe the probability of each spin on Spinner Y.

   a) spinning an even number _____

   b) spinning an odd number _____

4. Is spinning odd numbers more probable on Spinner X

   or Spinner Y? Explain. _____

   _____

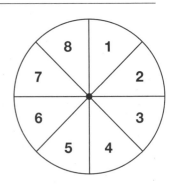

Spinner X

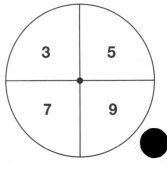

Spinner Y

118   Chapter 13: Probability

Copyright © 2004 Nelson

CHAPTER 13

3 Making Predictions

Goal Make predictions and design and carry out experiments.

1. **a)** Cut out 10 strips of paper. Write a boy's name on each of 5 strips. Write a girl's name on each of the other 5 strips. Put the 10 strips in a paper bag.

   b) Predict the number of girls' names and boys' names you will draw in 20 draws.

   girls' names _____ boys' names _____

   c) Draw a strip from the bag. Use the tally chart to record whether the strip has a boy's name or a girl's name. Put the strip back in the bag.

   d) Repeat part c) 19 times.

   e) Compare your results to your prediction.

   _____

   _____

2. In another experiment with 10 strips of names in a bag, you want drawing
   - a boy's name to be very probable
   - a girl's name to be very improbable

   a) Decide how many boys' names and how many girls' names you will use. Then make the strips to match what you decided. Put the 10 strips in a paper bag.

   b) Repeat parts b) to e) from Question 1.

   girls' names _____ boys' names _____

   c) Did your bag meet the conditions? _____

At-Home Help

The probability of a boy's name or a girl's name being drawn from a bag is related to how many of each are in the bag. The more girls' names there are, the higher the probability that a girl's name will be drawn.

Draw	Question 1 boy or girl	Question 2 boy or girl
1		
2		
3		
4		
5		
6		
7		
8		
9		
10		
11		
12		
13		
14		
15		
16		
17		
18		
19		
20		

4 Comparing Probabilities

Goal Make predictions and experiment with spinners with unequal sections.

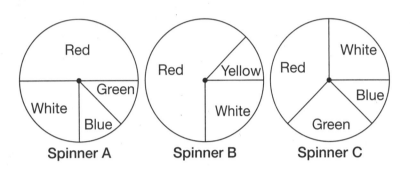

Spinner A   Spinner B   Spinner C

At-Home Help

The probability of landing on a spinner section is related to the size of the section. The larger the section, the more probable it will be to land on it.

1. On which spinner(s) is

  a) spinning yellow impossible? _____

  b) spinning green impossible? _____

  c) spinning green equally probable as spinning blue? _____

  d) spinning blue impossible? _____

2. Which spinner would you choose if spinning red wins a prize? _____

3. Which colour is equally probable on all 3 spinners? _____

4. Which colour(s)

  a) on Spinner A are impossible on Spinner B? _____

  b) on Spinner B is impossible on the other spinners? _____

  c) on Spinner A are equally probable? _____

  d) on Spinner C are equally probable? _____

5. Complete the probability line for Spinner A.

impossible   certain

CHAPTER 13

5 Creating Spinners

Goal Design spinners to meet given conditions and test the spinners.

1. Make the spinner match the conditions.

a)

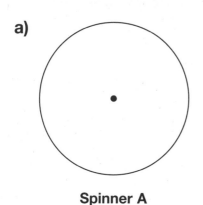

Spinner A

4 colours
all colours
equally probable

At-Home Help

The probability of landing on a spinner section is related to the size of the section. The larger the section, the more probable it will be to land on it.

b)

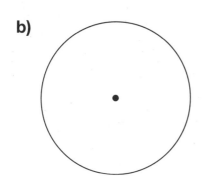

Spinner B

3 colours
red impossible

c)

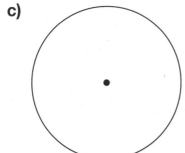

Spinner C

3 colours
2 colours equally probable
1 colour more probable

CHAPTER 13
6 Solve Problems Using Tree Diagrams

Goal Use tree diagrams to find all possible combinations.

1. The price of an ice-cream cone depends on the type of cone and the number of scoops.
   Cone: regular, waffle
   Scoops: 1, 2, 3

   a) Draw a tree diagram to list all possible combinations.

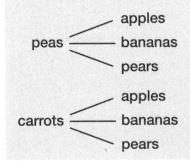

At-Home Help

A **tree diagram** can be used to list all possible combinations.

vegetables: peas, carrots
fruit: apples, bananas, pears

There are 6 possible combinations of 1 type of vegetable and 1 type of fruit.

b) How many different prices of ice-cream cones are there? _____

c) A person orders an ice-cream cone. Which is more probable?
   • A: The person orders a waffle cone with 2 scoops.
   • B: The person orders a regular cone with any number of scoops.

   Explain your choice. _____

   _____

   _____

Test Yourself

Circle the correct answer.

1. Which event is certain?

    A. It will rain tomorrow.

    B. We will have hot dogs for lunch this Wednesday.

    C. I will go to school this week.

    D. The class will go to the beach for a field trip.

2. Which event is possible, but unlikely?

    E. There will be snow in May.

    F. A new student will come into our class before the end of the year.

    G. July will be hot.

    H. The sun will rise tomorrow.

3. For Spinner X, which result is very unlikely for 20 spins?

    A. You land on odd numbers 11 times.

    B. You land 3 times on 6.

    C. You land 19 times on 8.

    D. You never land on 0.

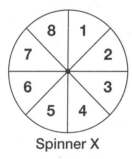
Spinner X

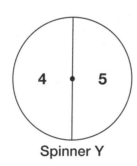
Spinner Y

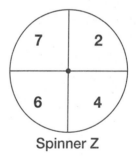
Spinner Z

4. For Spinner Z, which result is very likely for 20 spins?

    E. You land on odd and even numbers an equal number of times.

    F. You land on numbers that can be divided by 2.

    G. You land on numbers that are smaller than 5.

    H. You land 15 times on 7.

5. Which spinner would you choose if spinning an even number wins a prize?

    A. Spinner X   **B.** Spinner Y   **C.** Spinner Z   **D.** Spinner X or Y

6. Which spinner would you choose if spinning an odd number wins a prize?

    E. Spinner X   **F.** Spinner Y   **G.** Spinner Z   **H.** Spinner X or Y

1 Coordinate Grids

Goal Identify and describe locations on a grid.

1. Which community has each set of coordinates?

   a) B2 _____

   b) E4 _____

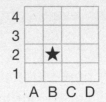

2. This walking trail has rest spots marked ®. Identify their coordinates.

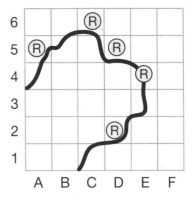

_____

3. Each player takes turns placing a counter on the grid. The first player to place 5 counters in a straight line wins.

   a) Name the coordinates for each ●.

   _____

   b) Name the coordinates for each ⊕.

   _____

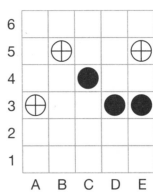

   c) Mark ● at D4 and ⊕ at A4. Mark ● at A5 and ⊕ at B2.

   d) What is the player using ● trying to do? _____

   _____

2 Translating Shapes

Goal Use and describe translations.

1. Which sets of shapes are **not** translations?

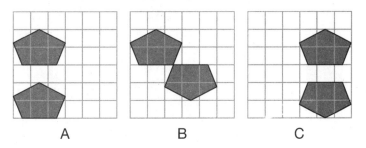

A   B   C

A. A and B   **C.** C and A

B. B and C   **D.** A, B, and C

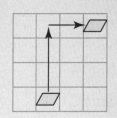
2. Draw the triangle for each translation. Label each triangle using the letter of its step.

Step **a**   Start at A4.

Step **b**   Translate 3 right and 2 down.

Step **c**   Translate 2 left and 4 up.

Step **d**   Translate 5 down and 3 right.

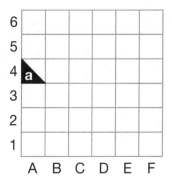

3. **a)** Which rectangle will be closest to B2 when translated 2 down and 1 left?

_____

   b) Where will rectangle **b** end up if it is translated 4 down and 3 left? Name the coordinates.

_____

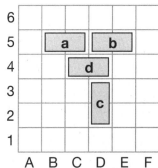

4. Describe translations of rectangle **a** to C1 and D1. Do not move it to grid squares with other rectangles.

_____

_____

3 Rotating Shapes

Goal Use and describe rotations.

1. Which sets of shapes are **not** rotations?

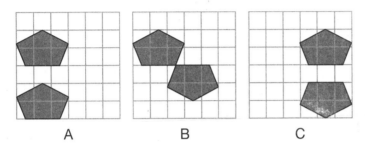

A   B   C

A. A and B   **C.** C and A

B. B and C   **D.** A, B, and C

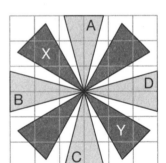
2. **a)** Describe the rotations of triangle A

to triangle B. _____

_____

b) Can the same rotation apply from triangle A

to triangle D? Explain. _____

_____

c) Describe 2 rotations of triangle X to triangle Y.

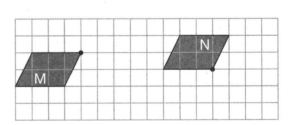

_____

_____

3. **a)** Rotate parallelogram M 90° CCW.

b) Rotate parallelogram N 180° CW.

c) Which rotation, a) or b), looks like

a translation? _____

d) Describe the translation. _____

4. **a)** Rotate the triangle 90° CCW 3 times.

b) What shape is created? _____

4 Reflecting Shapes

Goal Use and describe reflections.

1. Which sets of shapes are **not** reflections?

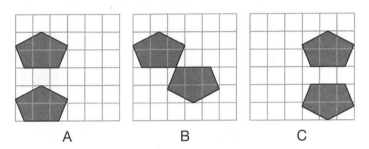

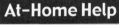

At–Home Help

A **reflection** of a shape is flipped to the opposite side of the line of reflection, staying the same distance from the line, not changing size or shape.

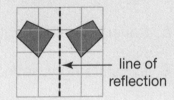

line of reflection

A. A and B   **C.** C and A

B. B and C   **D.** A, B, and C

2. Draw 3 reflections to show the whole tile design.

3. How are translations, rotations, and reflections the same? _____

_____

_____

_____

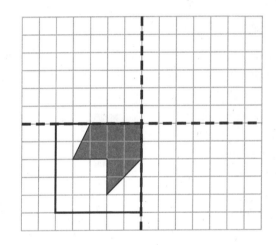

4. You can reflect a triangle several times to make a hexagon. The reflections are started here. Triangle A is reflected in a line through its right side to triangle B. Continue the reflections on the grid. Label each triangle with a different letter.

Describe each reflection. _____

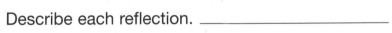

_____

_____

_____

5 Communicate About Transformations

Goal Describe translations, rotations, and reflections.

1. Which description is most accurate?

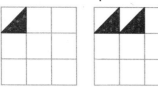 

Start   Step 1   Step 2   Step 3

At-Home Help

Communication Checklist
☑ Are your steps in order?
☑ Did you show enough detail?
☑ Did you include a diagram?
☑ Did you use math language?

A. translate, reflect, rotate

B. translate right, reflect, rotate CCW

C. translate 1 space right, reflect in line M, rotate about point P 180° CCW

D. translate 1 space right, reflect in line M, rotate about point P 90° CW

2. Karina described this transformation as "reflect in line M, rotate 180°, translate right."

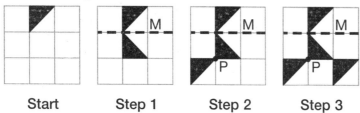

Start   Step 1   Step 2   Step 3

a) Describe the strengths of Karina's description.

_____

_____

b) Describe the parts of her description that need improvement.

_____

_____

c) Rewrite her description using your suggestions for improvement.

_____

_____

6 Transformation Patterns

Goal **Make patterns using transformations.**

1.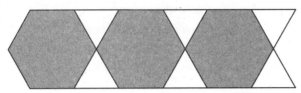

    a) What shapes are in this pattern?

    _____

    b) Describe the pattern in 2 different ways.

    _____

    _____

    _____

    _____

    _____

    _____

    _____

    _____

    _____

    _____

2. Create your own pattern on the grid below using these shapes.

7 Extending Transformation Patterns

Goal **Extend geometric patterns.**

1. a) Extend this pattern to complete the grid.

b) Describe the pattern using

transformations. _____

_____

_____

2. a) Extend this pattern to complete the grid.

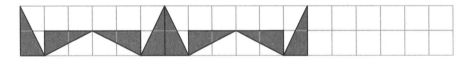

b) Describe the pattern using transformations. _____

_____

_____

3. a) Extend this pattern to complete the grid.

b) Describe the pattern using transformations. _____

_____

_____

Test Yourself

Circle the correct answer.

1. Which coordinates are marked on the BINGO card?

   A. B8, I16, G40, O53

   B. B8, I10, G43, O58

   C. B8, I18, G48, O51

   D. B8, I18, G40, O53

B	I	N	G	O
(8)	13	23	48	58
2	(18)	29	42	54
5	16	FREE	43	51
1	10	22	(40)	50
4	14	21	47	(53)

2. Where is the shape when it is translated 3 left and 2 down?

   E. A1

   F. A2

   G. B2

   H. B1

   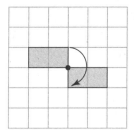

3. What are the angle and direction of the rotation shown?

   A. 90° CCW

   B. 90° CW

   C. 180° CW

   D. 180° CCW

4. Which shape is a reflection of shape A?

   E. shape B

   G. shape D

   F. shape C

   H. shape E

5. Which is the next shape in this pattern?

   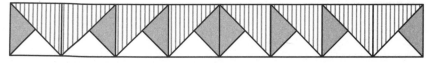

   A.

   B.

   C.

   D.